I

Am

Rock-Medicine

June 1, 1995

Ms. Elaine Nelson
San Jose, CA

Dear Elaine:

I just wanted to let you know how things have gone with my holding stones.

I started with the 7 cleansers plus petrified wood in April 1994. I also gave a set (basic cleansers) to my husband and to my mother. About 3-4 weeks later my mother asked me if it could have affected her arthritic pointer finger. She had no more pain. That relief has continued to this day although she no longer holds the stones.

My husband and I both suffered from a repeated fungal infection. We both had relief from that, which we attributed to the stones. In my case, it did not reappear (after coming monthly for years) until April 1995. I was still holding stones at that time too. It is again gone after appearing for two months. Additionally, I am holding stones for breast cancer. I have held several combinations since January 24, 1995. I am quite healthy at this time. I do many complimentary medical treatments as well. I also eat organic, mostly raw produce and juice every day. I enjoy holding my stones and have done it continually since I began in April 1994. I look forward to complete recovery, one way or the other.

Thanks, Elaine.

Sincerely,

Ann Fonfa
New York, N.Y. 10018
Chair, Alternative/Complimentary Therapies Committee for
SHARE, Self-Help for Women with Breast or Ovarian Cancer
F768-7185

I Am

Rock-Medicine

by
Sela Weidemann Randazzo

Lifeforce Publications
San Jose, California

Thank You Carolyn! Please use and share this book to the wellness of us all! Love, Sela

I Am Rock-Medicine

by

Sela Weidemann Randazzo

Published by Lifeforce Publications
First Edition June 1996

Cover Art by Peter Teekamp
Layout by Janet McEnroe
Printed by Cal Printing

ISBN 0-9653352-1-6

Dedication

This book is dedicated to all who hoped that the creator of love would intervene.
From those who believed it.

Acknowledgements

This 13 year work is the result of the following people's time:

To my mother, Viola Weidemann, I thank you for your sacrifice of sanity so that I might learn; To my Father, Warren Weidemann, I thank you for your spirit of innovation, inspiration and inventiveness. To my Mom, Diane, for your love. To Amber, Aimee and Brandon Gamble, for your loyalty. To Gail, Christina and Carrin for your consistency. To Bob Weir, Mickey Hart and Bill Kreutzman for your enthusiasm. To Jerry Garcia for playing the devil's advocate. To Gene and Pearl at TOPS Rock Shop for the opportunity to learn and provide quality minerals. To my Uncle Frank and Aunt Connie Weidemann for your clarity. To Judy MacLane for all your work. To Sloopy Barreau for all your energy and time. To Christine for your knowledge. To Nancy Worthington for Leonard. To Janet McEnroe for your computer sense and longevity of friendship. To Honey Bordas, Judy Cranmer, Tamar Hurwitz, Lana Chapman, Shirley Thompson, Alice Gilchrist, Cindy B., Char Castro, Pat Gardener Cindy Mulford, Theresa Day and Carola for your support and encouragement. Thanks to Bob Lewis at Gems Galore. To Bill Pruden of Olympic Mountain Gems for your vast mineral supply. To Lynn Gordon for your wonderful photo and your kindness. To the Wilsons for being so accommodating. To Elaine Nelson for completing the task, and Jeff Nelson for his faith and support. Finally, to my husand Micheal, thank you for being there.

And to the countless others who have used Rock Medicine

that we may all be more well as a whole.

About The Author

Sela Weidemann Randazzo has been practicing Rock-Medicine therapy for over thirteen years and she has been presenting classes and seminars for the last eight. Born in Philadelphia, she has lived all over the world. Sela was given the task of teaching Rock-Medicine to the masses because she asked for the job of helping the planet when she was just a small child. The strong conviction that her own well-being and that of others are mutually dependent upon each other causes her to be available for teaching or consultation whenever and wherever requested. Sela Weidemann, the name, literally translates to "rock shepherd".

Contents

The Stones (cont.)

Preface

Preface

The basic premise and intention of this book is to provide both a domestic use guide and a comprehensive medical text on the proper use and application of crystals and gemstones as tools for wellness.

These minerals are precision instruments capable of balancing to a state of "well being", one's mind, body, and spirit. As the human being is a delicate equation of all three, it is necessary to treat all three areas simultaneously when one is out of balance. All forms of imbalance equate to toxicity which, in turn, manifests as an illness.

You will probably find this as hard to believe as I do...and I'm the one who lived it. All my life I have felt that I would do something special. In fact, at the age of five I asked God to let me help this planet. The televised scenes of children starving, skeleton like, in the fund raiser videos caused me to really mean it. I grew to believe that it would probably be in the field of politics since there was no other arena that measured up to my inspiration for change. Little did I realize that what the Creator had in mind would literally rock nations. I can remember being five. Not many conscious memories exist for me any earlier than that. It is probably the best validation I have of the significant change that took place. It caused me to become someone different, a walk in, you might say. I can tell you the details of the very night it happened.

I was at my best friend's house. Her name was Maureen. She and I were in her family's rec room playing ping pong. All of a sudden in mid swing, I was stopped short by a clearly audible voice saying, "Your Mother wants you home." I knew immediately that not Maureen, nor her brother or Father, who were also in the room, had spoken. Nor had they heard it. I said aloud: "My Mother wants me home." This was not a statement that would cause any of them to be aware of what had and was taking place. As I lived close by, I set off alone for home. It was dusk. Night was falling fast. A combination of night blindness and dyslexia had me turned around and lost in minutes.

My parents had raised us intelligently and I knew my full name and address. I was not afraid. I also knew that I was in my own neighborhood. All the people's houses around me were my neighbors'. I went up to the closest doorway and knocked. No answer. Now it was dark. Instead of it occurring to me to try the next door, I panicked and felt very frightened.

I turned from the door and bolted towards the first of four steps leading to the sidewalk. As soon as I was at the edge of that top step I bumped into someone standing there. I looked up to see the face of Jesus. This was a familiar face and garb from every Sunday School picture I'd ever seen. He was just standing there. I was raised by a fanatically fundamentalist mother. With this intense biblical orientation the stories and miracles were real. I had been deeply ingrained in the perception of Jesus as a real human being who was my friend. In that light, my gut level reaction was one of relief. I knew in my understanding that if I was lost, Jesus was probably a very good person to have show up. There was no verbal communication. I *felt* his mind search mine. At the moment he established I was comfortable with the persona that was before me, he was no longer the same. All of a sudden he was not the familiar Christian manifestation but rather a total light being. In the next moment I was caught up in his arms and instantaneously in front of my own front door.

My mother was a mentally imbalanced woman whose illness went undetected in fanatical religious organizations. My father was a lawyer, a chemist and an electrical engineer. He was the individual who formulated unleaded gasoline at Atlantic Richfield Laboratories.

From that day and for about the next three years I found myself in a frequent state of tears. I remember sitting at the dinner table crying from such a profoundly deep place. My parents would ask me what was wrong. I could only answer them by saying that I could not explain it but that everything was really going to be all right. It was as if I was detached from my feelings. Although I was crying big crocodile tears, I did not feel sadness in my heart but rather duty. This, I later learned, was known as travail. This is the agonizing over the plight of all mankind.

The next major incident was when I was eight years old. We were members of a Pentecostal church in downtown Philadelphia, the city of brotherly love. While in the midst of a Sunday morning sermon as I looked around the sanctuary I saw every person in the building light up. It was like individual lights on a Christmas tree. Each person had a color surrounding their body. It was so vivid and obvious that it did not occur to me that I was the only one seeing it. I elbowed my mother and said, "look at that!" She responded quizzically and asked what I was talking about. I didn't take my eyes off the illuminated crowd and said, "That!...everyone is lit up with color!" She again asked what I was talking about. I was so frustrated by the possibility that she did not see it that I responded with exasperation. "Our minister is glowing with a lime green light.", I said.

The next thing I knew I was being rushed down the isle to the alter at the stage. This was not to cast the demons out of me but rather to proclaim me as a child prophet. I was learning that it was not the best idea to let anyone know what was happening to me. That you do not let other people know when these things happen. We ended up at the preacher's home for dinner. He got to revel in his color. Mother got to be in the special holy spotlight. I was disgusted. I was torn between the comfortable absurdity of my mother's church group and the knowledge that I was being singled out for incredible communication with our Creator. I chose to be temporarily sucked in by the promise of rapture, or at very least salvation. I even took my ten dollars of birthday money and gave it all to the collection plate the following Sunday. It took me three trys to be sure I had the minister's eye as I gave it. This was definitely my mistake. In the instant that my gift was realized from the pulpit I knew that the value of what I had offered was lost. I was giving for the value's sake and not for the giving's sake.

The feeling of specialness dwindled in the years between eight and ten. Then one late fall day it was reborn. My older sister, her best friend and I were dragging a bale of hay across a field in our wagon home to our dog's house. As we reached the center of the open field all of a sudden we were aware of a ship....a space ship. It was perfectly still, only sixty feet above our heads. It was so close the detail is still deeply embedded in my memory. When we looked up, we all saw the under-belly of the ship clearly. We had been walking in daylight when we left the farm with the hay. Now we were looking up through pitch darkness at the lights and siding of a spacecraft. If there were rivets connecting the individual panels of metal we could have seen them. There were neat seams. There were no rivets. This encounter was so spectacularly close that the three of us did not speak about it for almost ten years.

My sisters and I were living through a nightmare of physical and mental abuse. What we did not fear from my mother, we feared from her ever more radical church groups. I had the benefit of this audible voice guiding me and to this day the results of our cruel childhood can be seen vividly in my three sisters. It is as if someone altogether different raised me. They did.

When my father died I was thirteen. It was the first time that I had been allowed my own room. I was always the one who had to share a room with one of my sisters and the night my father died I was in my bed. Movement in a picture of the little shepherd boy caught my attention. It all of a sudden had become animated, life-like, with subtle movement of the boy and the lamb in his arms. As my attention was drawn to the picture I did not notice from where my father came. I was now aware of his full physical presence at my bedside. He said in a telepathic way that he had been allowed to come and say good-bye to only me. As I rose up out of my bed he said I may not touch him. I followed him down the hallway from my room. Instead of turning the corner he disappeared into the wall. The fact that I had risen up out of bed to participate in this encounter let me know that it was an actual occurrence and not a dream.

Just a few months later my sisters and I found ourselves on a fifteen acre religious cult campground. Our mother told us we were there for a three week camp. One month later she informed us that our estate in Pennsylvania had been put up for sale and we were going to live here. We were registered into the local school. I was moved from seventh grade to ninth grade and was cutting school four out of five days while remaining an "A" student. We girls were four little princesses moved from absolute wealth to abject poverty. The two room cabin we moved into had no indoor plumbing and we had to navigate a swamp and an electrified pony fence to reach the outhouse.

The voice that I had heard since the age of five on a daily basis had never left me. It was not until the age of sixteen that I realized that not everyone was hearing this voice. This comforting voice never told me anything strange or harmful. It taught me that having a physically and mentally abusive parent was not the result of my being good or bad but rather that of my mother being ill.

The campground was one continuous nightmare of physical and emotional abuse. The majority of abuse came from my mother or under her sanctioning. At the age of sixteen I finally left home and went out into the world on my own. The spirit continued to speak to me.

Sela Weidemann was the name given me at birth. Literally translated, it means "rock shepherd". This fact did not come to my attention until many years after my work with the mineral kingdom had begun.

Thirteen years ago, I attended a conference in Detroit on metaphysics;. As I was a novice to such offered topics as advanced astrology, numerology, and the tarot, I opted to sit in on the only presentation offered to a beginning student. The subject matter was healing with gemstones and was presented by a woman in Larkspur, California. The method by which we were taught to determine appropriate usage of the individual stones is called kinesiology;, or muscle testing;. This is a widely used and accepted testing method amongst physicians and therapists. In simple terms, the subject's own muscle strength or weakness is used to obtain accurate indication from his subconscious, as to which may be contraindicated because of allergy; or just misapplication.

After about five years of utilizing this practice, I began to see combinations of stones being repeated consistently for the same maladies. This cross referencing gave me the standardization of the use of about thirty stones.

In early 1987, I spontaneously began "channeling" or receiving audibly, the specific usage of another seventy or so stones. This gracious intervention by a "higher source of knowledge" was, in effect, emergency measures. The Creator saw that we as a people have all but destroyed our earthly kingdoms and ourselves with it.

The polluting of our waters, air, and soil have rendered the vegetable kingdom toxic. You cannot treat something toxic with something toxic. Our planet life from which we derive most of our medicinal products is becoming virtually useless as a means by which we can obtain health. With the onset of the atomic age, we were then putting our mineral kingdom at risk by the effects of radiation. The mineral kingdom is our last available source for healing ourselves and the planet. This is a conclusion that clinical science would have reached for itself, but not before too much damage was done to the Earth's mineral resources. As a result of these circumstances, and my request to be of assistance, the art and science of stone medicine was born.

That the mineral kingdom is recognized as a viable means of healing is an ever broadening reality. History substantiates this kingdom's work record. The very names of individual stones sometimes were given them because of their healing virtues. We see countless examples of ancient Egyptian tombs safeguarding the remains of the dead, as well as the amulets and beads which were used to treat them while alive. Prophetic references to this kingdom's usage, both past and present, are well documented in virtually all teachings of theology and alchemy.

It is my firm belief that the ancient loss of the practical usage of these instruments was due to the greed of those to whom the original knowledge was imparted. It is also my belief that the biblical reference to Christ's words concerning the "rocks and stones crying out to bear witness to the power of the Creator, at a time when mankind has ceased to glorify creation," is speaking about this inception of Rock-Medicine's introduction here and now.

There is no mystery here. This volume presents all the channeled information received to date. The maladies chosen to be addressed first are a composite of our world's current needs and heaven's own.

Many great minds are bringing about the uniting of hearts and turning their convictions true to unconditional love, a source of harmonious delight. Happiness, health, and camaraderie are the combined riches of heaven on earth. This planet has provided for the survival of life here. Our use of the available tools guarantees the quality of that life. Stone medicine and its introduction into the daily lives of us all can be likened to a purge of fire. The vast mineral kingdom represents the molten veins of the early formation of the earth.

The animal, vegetable, and mineral kingdoms are all relative to one another, as are the mind, body, and soul of an individual. Likewise, each of us is individually reflective to each other. Given this oneness, the health of one affects the wellness of all. In this light, we see the logic in evolution presenting us with the means to detox an extremely toxic existence because of the only kingdom (or tools) left untainted. We can treat the common cold or AIDS. We can use this science as healing or preventive measures. The only requirement for these minerals to be effective is that they must be used. The methods are simple and few. Essences rendered from gemstones are practically as obtainable and affordable as the water of which they are made.

Stones and rocks have been gathered by many, many more people than know how they work. This is the best of all possible situations, to have the masses gathering about themselves the cherished means of utilizing vibrational influences, just as the instructions are yet arriving. We did and somehow do know this mineral kingdom and its worth. Magic is not the miracle of power, but that of creative desire. When creative desire is given vibrational energy, it becomes a manifestation.

You may well ask here why we do not all just use our inherent mental abilities to manifest a peaceful and healthy world? This is one way of accomplishing this world goal. Unfortunately, too many people are ill of mind, body, and spirit to facilitate the use of their wills to bring about these major changes. Stone medicine is the method by which we will heal ourselves to a point of truly utilizing our own individual power skills to their fullest potential. In the past, medical science has been hampered in their attempts to standardize treatments and cures. In many cases (cancer and arthritis, for example) we find inconsistency in the effectiveness of the treatments. What sometimes works, but does not always is an extremely tenuous way to approach healing. Just as a balanced hammer always drives a straight nail home, when the tools are properly used, stone medicine always elicits a constant result.

When properties of any kind converge as a result of the evolution of life, it is harmonic. This occurrence, on August 17, 1987, was the birth of the mineral's vibrations for the new age. There was a coming together of energy and light that was celebrated around the world; many more than understood gathered and danced, prayed, meditated, and participated in a global harmony. This action prompted an act of faith and hope for bonding the life forces of the planet with new strength and wellness.

Since that moment, many monumental occurrences have caused dramatic change. Global weather patterns and geological motions are being related to us now on a daily basis. New political freedoms are being orchestrated in Russia, Germany, and the Middle East. The use and observation by the masses of Rock-Medicine will be another. There is a resounding need world-wide for a more comprehensive and available means of medical self help.

When you consider the word holy you also get the word "whole". This is the dictionary's interpretation. In other words, all that is not well is ill and as we all are part of each other and the planet then no one can truly be well until we all are. Now, the best description of Creator I can offer is this: the combination of Truth and Self-discipleship always produces a state of unconditional love. This is the "God is Love" theory. Self-discipleship is as being true to one's self or person; true to its needs and desires. Self's base need and desire are health. From this, all happiness is derived.

Nothing is more a term of scientific thought than the word TRUTH. There is no greater power on earth than that of the mind (or self). Enlightenment by awareness that we are all one and of the same is self-discipleship at its truest form.

Right now the planet and its atmosphere are toxic, likewise, the animal and vegetable kingdoms. Only deep inside the rock of ages do we find untainted vibration. This has been kept safe there for us. All over the world and in every culture are the threads that keep conscious connection with their knowledge, until such a time as humankind used them in their mature state; as should any of the things existing in this garden we are tending be used.

Crystals, rocks, gemstones, fossils, metals, and even crystallized saps, such as amber;, make up the vast array of precision vibrational instruments used in Rock-Medicine. Even as the time-space continuum flows us through the changes we see antiquation as we advance. So it is true of the applications of the stones. Some, if not most of, the ancient standards are no longer applicable and have evolved to a different correlation to the planet, her atmosphere, and her inhabitants. Some minerals have gained in their resonant strength to a point of being a certain danger, if used improperly. When one obtains an awareness as to the proper handling of the mineral influences in one's surroundings, there is an automatic obligation to learn the potential risks, safeguards, and antidotes related to these energies. This kingdom is not, however, set up to be used in any heinous or malicious manner.

"I AM Rock-Medicine" presents the aspects of origin, history, practice, safe-guards, essence making, and methodology of this material. We wish you delight and wisdom as this great work of ours proceeds. We are our own best aspect and resource. A new age level of our repetition of resources will serve to reawaken the skills of research, study, and development of cosmic existence. A computer-like higher mind is being linked to us on a conscious level; our socioeconomic convictions bear witness to this Peace is a popular demand. Peace of mind is happiness; peace of body is health; peace of soul is freedom. The truest of freedoms is free-flow. One such practice is out-of-body travel. Astral-projection is only one of the precursors to our evolving in ourselves the skills of telepathy, teleportation, telekinesis, and astral travel.

In this course, a known truth or conscious truth is called knowledge.

Knowledge in itself remains moot until a demonstrative vibration causes it to become wisdom. As cause and effect go, wisdom perpetrates life's survival, growth, and improvement. As has been said: "the wise man has the power".

Another timely analogy is the phrase from a Van Morrison song: "If I could teach my heart to think and my head to feel". This is a just description of the current enlightening by the Spirit. Our hearts' desires are being raised to our minds and pushing the mental energy flow upward physically and emotionally. The spirit is doing as well as the mind and body are and to the same degree.

Many forms of exercise were incorporated into the education of being one with all to introduce us to a state of total awareness. The various meditative practices were all for the furthering of our progress towards a state of grace, or a divine state. The harmony of matter is in constant motion. Many of these simple exercises have been built into dogmas, doctrines and icons of worship instead of the tools they are meant to be.

There are no mantras, prayers, incantations, or ceremonies in the practical application of Rock-Medicine. It is a very simple and basic system to use. The only actions necessary to the patient's being receptive is that the medicine must be used as prescribed. Special care must be and has been used in the sharing of this understanding and practice. We suggest that you read this text in full, and that you use it with a working knowledge, in other words, with wisdom.

The Great Work

The Great Work

There are multitudes of volumes written on these changing times. Some call this period one of planetary transition We are talking about simple and basic change. Humankind has already begun to swing the value system or the quality of life towards an enlightened existence due to the overwhelming desire of the masses for peace. With this desire comes an automatic response to the plight of those unfortunates who are without water, food, shelter, and clothing. There are ever-increasing numbers of individuals rising to contribute to meet these needs by others near and far.

Just as the single child is getting the assistance it needs to grow in a productive manner, so too, has the very planet received "care-packages" of information to expedite the salvation of this growth and well being. Rock-Medicine is the means by which all things toxic may be cleared to their states of balance.

We are all connected by way of mind, body and spirit. Although, we can do all things by way of our minds' powers and abilities, we must be in top working order to do so. This makes the wellness of each one of us the responsibility of us all. In other words, where there is found one brother or sister among you who has an illness or imbalance, so also do you. This realization takes the idea of health care out of the previously encumbered realm of confidentiality.

Rock-Medicine has the unique quality of being able to be administered effectively to another whether they accept it, want it, believe it, or even know it! This clinical application for the ills and ails of others is but one aspect of the clean-up measures known as the Great Work. From this place of well-being however, come automatically those inclinations towards turning the tide on the current trend of waste and abuse of the earth and its resources.

There are no exceptions to the rule that all are in need of healing, just as there are no exceptions to the fact that the health of all is the responsibility of us all.

Foremost in the path of enlightenment is the realization that all elements given by and derived from the Mother Earth have a purpose. All things are tools and instruments set here for our use. There is a high degree of misuse of a great number of these. This is due to a lack of proper knowledge of application. We hide from taking care. Most of the things we do are state altering whether it be T.V. or ingesting chemicals, it could be chanting, dancing or merely breathing. We see much in the way of denial of the reality of our world's situation. So many people abuse drugs and alcohol, using them as crutches and hiding places rather than in their intended capacity as means of enhancing celebration and of altering perspectives to expand creativity. Since we as people naturally tend towards extremes, instead of learning moderation in the use of these powerful influences, we have developed the equal and opposite mentality that total abstinence is the only answer. This "baby-proofing" scenario holds control of our own lives at bay just as does the ignorant over-indulgence. In other words, to use or not use any mode of mind-altering tool should be a decision based on evaluation and choice, and not one of fear. This guideline is an analogy of reference that can be applied to a vast degree of other areas inclusive of incantations, meditations, food-stuffs, and of being our brother's keeper. Religious indoctrination is equally based in fear and denial of one's connection to the whole. True freedom is the love of making moment-to-moment decisions based upon the moment-to-moment changes in the personal environment. This breeds flow.

The Great Work is the demonstrative role taken by all to involve themselves in the detoxification of the planet's mind, body and spirit as well as our own. This is what is necessary to allow the Creator's divine presence to return and fully abide with this plane on a full-time basis, thus giving back to us our state of grace or heaven on earth.

Looking at the list of available stones and their uses is self-explanatory as to what is required in the way of addressing the imbalance of our current existence. First, of course, would be the obvious individual cases of medical need. Next, we have to deal with the dangerous level of radiation toxicity planet-wide. For this, we can set up systems of long-distance spreads using cobalt. Next, the air pollution for which we use a combination of clear quartz, white quartz, and pyrite. This again is where we administer by way of a long-distance spread. You may use either a single stone compiled of these three elements or set the three stones together. Water pollution is going to take a bit more preparation and involvement. To get the stones' vibrations in the necessary form for application, we must first render an essence of smokey quartz in some contained water and then add the essence to the bodies of water and systems. In order to obtain and then maintain a non-toxic environment, it will be optimal to be able to utilize our current advances in technology and set a vast long-distance spread in orbit around the planet. This will obviously require the assistance, cooperation and large-scale involvement by the governments of the earth. This can only be expected when the true scientific nature of the practice and studies of Rock-Medicine are adopted by the masses. This awareness is coming in rapidly. Your participation by way of the use of this domestic text for the health and improvement of your households and communities will facilitate its manifestation.

Applications

Of

The Stones

Methods Of Application

Rock-Medicine works by way of electromagnetic vibration at a chemical level. The methods of application are quite simple. The hardest part about doing this therapy is remembering to do it faithfully for at least three weeks. After twenty-one days of consistent use, it is important that you see your physician and get re-evaluated.

If medication is being used, those choices and amounts will change. In the cases of the use of synthesized chemicals, such as lithium or insulin, levels should be tested daily or at least with dramatically increased frequency.

Obviously, there is much generality in the guideline of the three week time table. Some situations may require only brief assistance of mere hours or days. This would be true of everything from irritating insect bites or rashes to the common cold or allergy attack. Then on the other hand, depending upon the patient's age, duration of illness and its severity, the application may require many months. This would be true in the case of cataracts or bringing one's vision back to 20-20.

There are four main methods of application: 1) Hand held 2) Essence 3) Focus Direct 4). From the first to the fourth, they go in order of ability as far as being able to bring the most expeditious healing. Hand holding the stones is the best. Not very far behind is essence. A focus direct is quite a bit less expeditious as finally is the blanket spread, which requires months to match results obtained from holding the stones themselves for days.

Hand Held

All stones combined for the specific imbalance being addressed are held together in the proper hand. For men, it is the left hand and for women, it is the right. This is consistent with the body's directional flow of energy. A woman's flow comes in through her right hand and out her left. A man's flow comes in through his left hand and out his right. Regardless of one's sexual orientation, the chromosomal pattern designating male and female is the basis determining which hand is used.

The stones are held for twenty minutes four times a day. If the time exceeds twenty minutes, you run the risk of over saturating the stones with the toxins they are drawing from you. The result will be the voiding of that application, but will not make you any sicker than you are. I find it helpful to set my timer at eighteen minutes to insure against running the treatment too long.

After the time is up, set the stones aside to clear. They may be put in your pocket or in a bag around your neck, just as long as they are not in direct contact with your skin. They may be put on any non-metallic surface and will clear themselves within three hours. It is advised that they not be placed to clear on any appliance that is plugged into an electrical socket.

It is not necessary to do anything but leave them alone. No sunlight, moonlight, or salt cleansing makes any difference. In fact, using salt or salt water is detrimental to your mineral tools as it has a caustic effect on them. This practice is an "old wife's tale". It originates from when sages and shamans of old carried their stones and crystals from place to place on their back with their ration of food and good drinking water. They stopped periodically to wash the dust off. When by the coast, they used the salty sea water as opposed to using their precious drinking water. It was a matter of practicality that has been blown out of proportion.

Just as our own bodies grow a new top layer of skin over a given period of days, so the stones cleanse themselves by completing a full revolution or cycle in their atomic substance in a matter of three hours.

Three to four hours after setting the stones to clear, the twenty minute treatment is repeated. This is to be done four times in each day. Up to six hours may go between treatments.

The body's most natural method of healing is rest. Therefore, it is not conducive to wellness to interrupt one's sleep to do this. Four well-spaced applications from rising to bedtime are sufficient.

The best form of stones to use is rough, uncut, and unpolished. But, the first rule of thumb is "use what you have versus not bringing the healing". Even if your application requires amethyst, for example, an amethyst in a piece of jewelry will do as long as it is not set in silver.

This is the strongest, most expeditious means of administering Rock-Medicine. Using Rock-Medicine is akin to the way that prescription antibiotics work. When the rock vibration encounters an ailing area, the stone boosts it up to its well points. After three to four hours, it begins dropping back down to an ill or low resonance level. Then you come in with the next application. Over time, these repetitive intervals of help act like a parent helping a child ride his two wheeler. The balance is learned and holds its own.

Essence

An essence is rendered by placing cleared stones in a glass bowl, jar, or tumbler filled with water. Put your combination in the water for at least three to four hours (the full revolution time). I always opt to set my essence overnight to insure a solid rendering. Cover to prevent dust settling in it.

When all stones have air bubbles on them, this is your application in the water through oxygen exchange.

There are some stones which are water soluble or occur in a powdery or crumbly state that prohibits their use in an essence. Use common sense to insure that no residual particles settle into your essence. If your instrument is water soluble, you must employ the means of "setting" a clear quartz crystal to be that stone and use the crystal to render your essence. (See clear quartz crystal)

The stones are then removed from the water. Whether a bathtub full or a cupful, the water is full strength essence. Essence must not be diluted by more than three to one three parts water or other liquid, to one part essence. Essence, as well as the two following applications, enables us to treat someone without their even being aware of the application, and works just as well as if they use if for themselves. This type of circumstance is limitless the addict, the angry, the mean, the prejudiced, the non-believer in wellness and all other types of self-destructive imbalances.

Essence works well in a baby's bottle. If the patient is required to take nothing by mouth, per physicians' orders, the essence may be applied by drops to the forehead or wrists, though it is not as effective as when ingested.

The standard application of essence is four drops held under the tongue briefly before swallowing. The capillaries under the tongue are very close to the surface and absorb essence quickly into the bloodstream. This is repeated four times a day at the same three to six hour intervals, for a minimum of three weeks. Again the duration of treatment is directly related to the severity and prolongation of the illness.

Essence should be stored in an amber or dark colored dropper bottle which is available at most pharmacies. If volume essence is made, you may want to refrigerate it to avoid algae growing in the water. Since the rock-vibration is non-organic, it is not necessary to use any type of catalyst, suspender, or preservative.

Focus Direct

In order to work a focus direct, the first thing required is a quartz crystal with a perfect point. This means no chips, no cracks, and no mutilation of any kind. When a stone or stones are set against the base or sides of a clear quartz crystal, the stones' vibration travels along the body of the crystal, and like a turbo charger, is forced into the smaller and smaller space to be emitted as a "beam" of that stone or stones energy. This laser like gun can be directed at any individual and will be as an application of Rock-Medicine. This beam will not travel through walls or glass or turn corners. If anyone steps between the beam and its intended goal, that person will then be its affected target.

If a cluster of quartz crystals are used, a beam will be coming out of each and every perfect point on the cluster. This is an excellent tool to use in any home, office, classroom, or work place.

Choose stones to be used carefully. Use common sense and know exactly what each stone does.

The focus direct sends the beam(s) a distance directly proportional to the weight of the piece of quartz used. That distance is approximately one hundred feet per pound (fifty feet-one half pound, twenty-five feet-one quarter pound etc.).

The focus direct is much less expeditious in its ability to heal completely than the essence or hand held method.

Stones used in an essence of focus direct or spread need no clearing time as they are not in physical contact with any toxins. If stones are held, they must be cleared before using in any of the other three methods or hand held by someone else for treatment.

Blanket Spread

The blanket spread is also generated through clear quartz crystal. The crystal or crystals used need not be clean or transparent nor have good points or termination. Place stones for combination against the clear quartz crystal on any sides, just as long as all stones touch the crystal(s). Surround all this with a ring of lapis. This can be a strand of beads or single pieces placed touching each other, to form a circle or ring, or a circle or ring of small quartz crystals with one piece of lapis in it. The quartz crystals touching the other pieces will transmit the single piece of lapis' vibration around the ring. A blanket spread treats in a full radius of one hundred miles per pound of quartz in the center. Its influence goes up, down, and all around from the spread, transcending walls, roofs, floors, etc. This is the method by which we may treat cities, continents and the globe. (Illustrations of focus direct and blanket spread next page.)

Rock-Medicine is a precision technology. Just as with clinical medicine, treating two different maladies at a time may not always be advised. Always treat in priority order beginning with the most serious situation first. If you need to treat two illnesses or injuries running concurrently you may take your application as essence or hand held for one and then, with a completely different and specific combination, treat the second. You may do this one application right after another but they must be done in full and separate from one another. When treating physical maladies this applies to all four forms of application. This is because the stones work with electromagnetic vibration. In other words they "speak" to each other carrying messages for directing the combination much like letters or numbers. If your combination is telling the stones to go to the area of the spinal column and at the same time you are holding stones that denote attention to the balance of blood sugar you will be confusing the stones. Just as if you were told to go to two places at the same time, the stones are unable to go in any direction when given two different chemical messages simultaneously.

Rock-Medicine forms a sentence. With each stone you add to that sentence you will be directing the healing vibration to what is wrong and where it is located. You will start virtually every combination with the general cleansers which are jade, amber, smokey quartz, pyrite, hematite (or carnelian), old clay and covellite. From there you determine which part of the body is effected, tissue, nerve, muscle, bone etc., and add the proper stones accordingly. It is highly recommended in the event of multiple maladies that you start the first three weeks with just the general cleansers. After the three weeks are up re-evaluate the condition and establish what remains and then proceed by treating in priority order with specific combinations.

When you first begin to use the stones your system will experience rapid detoxification on all levels. It is common to have several hours of flu-like symptoms a few days into treatment. The body will eliminate toxins through whatever orifices are most convenient.

Most importantly it is always necessary that you get initial diagnosis from a qualified medical professional. When one is on prescribed medication such as insulin, lithium, blood pressure, thyroid, etc., you must be checked by your physician with dramatically increased frequency to have those levels adjusted as the body heals.

The Use Guide

Master Blend

In the serious pursuit of wellness it is necessary to treat not only the symptoms of illness but the causes or catalyst. Over the years we have had many experiences where we have combined the specific stones for a single malady. In countless instances where the prescribed application was administered the malady itself would disappear. However, a secondary illness would surface elsewhere. In treating that second condition we found a repetition of the same process.

This led us to the obvious conclusion that we were not addressing the areas of distress, which initially allow us to experience the inception of imbalances. These imbalances include everything from accident to attitude to illness. We have formulated a combination which we are calling the master blend. It is this combination that we feel will enable us to do the most complete cleansing for the purpose of eradicating any and all predispositions to imbalance. The complete list includes thirty-three stones and incorporates the seven physical cleansers as well. The master blend list is as follows:

Adamite	Coal	Labradorite
Agate	Covellite	Lapis
Amazonite	Diamond	Onyx
Amber	Dinosaur Bone	Petrified Wood
Aventurine	Gold	Pyrite
Carnelian	Granite	Rose Quartz
Celestite	Hematite	Selenite
Citrine	Hemmimorphite	Smokey Quartz
Chrysocolla	Jade	Sodalite
Chrysoprase	Jasper	Sugelite
Clay	Kunzite	Topaz

Use Guide

Add to the **master blend** stones when indicated in the following list:

Adhesions - amethyst, halite, rhodocrosite

Aggression- aragonite, bornite

AIDS- heliotrope,. amethyst

Alcoholism- amethyst

Allergies- amethyst, galena
       eyes- fluorite, malachite
       nose- fluorite, sharks tooth
       rash- rhodocrosite

Alzheimer's- lepidolite, amethyst

Anemia- amethyst, apatite

Anorexia- amethyst, apatite

Anxiety

Arthritis- halite, sulfur, amethyst, chrysoprase

Asthma- galena

Atrophy- amethyst, halite

Blood pressure- garnet

Bone damage- amethyst, coral

Brain- lepidolite, amethyst
       chemical imbalance
       fluid on - fluorite
       tumor - rhodocrosite

Bronchitis- amethyst, galena, black tourmaline, watermelon or pink tourmaline

Burns- topical application of honey, amethyst, rhodocrosite

Calcium deposits- amethyst, coral

Cataracts- malachite

Use Guide continue on next page

Cancer- amethyst, rhodocrosite, chrysoprase
       bladder- yellow or orange calcite
       breast- blue calcite, pearl
       cervical- white calcite, pearl
       colon- green calcite
       kidney- yellow or orange calcite
       leukemia- pink or red calcite
       lung- white calcite, black tourmaline, watermelon or pink tourmaline
       lymphoma- blue calcite
       ovarian- white calcite
       skin- white calcite
       spleen- green calcite
       stomach- green calcite
Candida- barite, moldavite, amethyst
Cardiac- amethyst, cinnabar, halite
Complexion- amethyst, rhodocrosite
Concussion- amethyst, lepidolite, rhodocrosite, wulfenite
Cuts- a topical application of honey, amethyst, rhodocrosite
Dental- aquamarine, amethyst
       gums- rhodocrosite
       teeth- coral
Depression- amethyst, lepidolite
Diabetes- green tourmaline, watermelon tourmaline or pink, amethyst
       insulin dependent- diopside
Divorce Trauma- ruby
Domesticity- abalone, aragonite, ulexite
Ears- amethyst, wood opal
Eating disorders- apatite
Emphysema- galena, black tourmaline, watermelon or pink tourmaline
Endomitrosis- amethyst, pearl, rhodocrosite
Epilepsy- amethyst, lepidolite
Fatigue- tigers eye
Fear- azurite, malachite
Female hormone balance- amethyst, pearl
Fever- amethyst
Flu- amethyst, chrysoprase
       ear- wood opal
       nose- sharks tooth
       throat- herkimer diamond
       stomach- green calcite

Fluid- amethyst, fluorite
     knee- sulfur
     lungs- black tourmaline, watermelon or pink tourmaline
     retention- apatite

Frigidity- ruby, pearl

General cleansing- amethyst

Goiter- amethyst, herkimer diamond, blue calcite

Grief

Headache

Hemophilia- amethyst, garnet

Hepatitis- amethyst

Herpes- amethyst, rhodocrosite

Impotence- amethyst, bornite, ulexite

Infertility- ivory
     physical- amethyst, pearl
     emotionally

Infidelity- ulexite

Inflammation- amethyst
     joints- sulfur
     muscle- halite

Insecurity

Inspiration- hessonite garnet, obsidian, red beryl

Irritability

Itching- amethyst, rhodocrosite

Kindness

Larynx- amethyst, herkimer diamond

Male hormone balance- amethyst, bornite, ulexite

Menopause- amethyst, pearl

Mononucleosis- amethyst, tigers eye

Multiple Sclerosis- amethyst, lepidolite, rhodocrosite

Muscles- amethyst, halite

Muscular Dystrophy- amethyst, halite

Neurological disorders- amethyst, rhodonite
     back - emerald
     body - rhodocrosite
     brain - lepidolite

Nightmares

Obesity- amethyst, apatite, rhodocrosite

Osteoporosis- amethyst, coral, emerald

Ovarian Cysts- amethyst, pearl, rhodocrosite

Pain- chrysoprase
Pleurisy- amethyst, fluorite, black tourmaline, watermelon or pink tourmaline
PMS- pearl
       bloating- amethyst, fluorite
       cramping- chrysoprase
       irritability

Pneumonia- amethyst, fluorite, black tourmaline, watermelon or pink tourmaline
Prejudice
Prenatal care- amethyst, mica
       brain chemical- lepidolite
       bone development- coral
       heart- cinnabar
Prepubescent trauma-
       sexual- ruby

Radiation toxicity- amethyst
Rape trauma- ruby
Self control
Self esteem
Spine- amethyst, coral, emerald
Stress
Suicidal tendencies- magnetite
Throat- amethyst, herkimer diamond
Thyroid- amethyst
Truthfulness
Vocal chords- amethyst, herkimer diamond
Voice box- amethyst, herkimer diamond
Wastefulness

The Stones

Abalone

Abalone is for domestic maturity.

This ocean offering of rainbows was once used by the Apache Indians during puberty ceremonies for adolescent girls. As the role of women in society has evolved, so too, has the pertinence of domestic maturity being a non-gender quality. Men as well as women are coming into a new awareness of taking a maternal outlook on life in their homes and communities. This quality of care taking is inclusive of organizational skills as well as feeling at ease with the domestic chores and perceptions of cleanliness.

Cleanliness as applied to the physical mode is pretty self-explanatory. In terms of mental and spiritual cleanliness, it is the promotion of comfort in one's abode. It is like fitting yourself and your energies in the home-space in an orderly fashion. This facilitates a smooth-running household without becoming obsessive on the one hand or lackadaisical on the other. Bear in mind that the literal observance of domesticity is not the same as fidelity to the family unit. Domestic maturity is the comfort and ease with which one executes the responsibilities of a well-run home while keeping priorities in their proper order. Keeping a clean and orderly space for your body and possessions affords efficiency in physical undertakings as does keeping the same degree of care for the mental and spiritual home.

Adamite

Adamite is for the elimination of blame.

Blame should not be confused with the concept of cause. When obstacles arise in one's life, it is important to see the causes in order to rise above them. However, from the beginning of man's fall from wellness, there has been an overwhelming tendency to lay blame in the course of dealing with one's problems. The first example we have of this syndrome is the story of the Garden of Eden. When asked whether or not he had eaten of the fruit of the Tree of the Knowledge of Good and Evil, Adam didn't give a simple yes-or-no answer, but rather qualified his mistake as somehow being the fault of Eve and laid the blame on her. She, in turn, did blame the serpent. That same scenario is repeated in every walk of life right up to today where we blame others for undesirable political, economic, and environmental conditions. The bottom line should be, "where do we stand at present, and where do we go from here?"

Rock-Medicine is here to deal with the vast array of imbalances afflicting this planet and its peoples. To be concerned with who and what is at fault for the present conditions would take as much time as all of history to date and would not repair it. Likewise, in dealing with the blame factors involved in interpersonal relationships and their failures, it is a waste of precious time and energy. There are only lessons to be learned from inappropriate actions by yourselves and others. As we enter the understanding of being one with all things, blame becomes a moot point of consideration. Growth is promoted by observation of potentials. We learn just as much from mistakes as from successes. It is not possible to live long enough for every individual to make every mistake personally. The planet would never have survived. So, instead, some beings contracted to emulate grave acts and attitudes of injustice and harm to be seen by others and learned from. In this light, it becomes easy to find love in your heart for that abusive parent, that lying lover, the baboon-ish politician, and the Hitlers of the world. Because their divine selves contracted to appear here in this existence to act as blatant examples of how not to be, we are still here and have been given the opportunity to act upon the lessons of life and set standards to insure our survival and growth. As in observing the great sacrifices of beloved leaders so that our burdens were lighter, so too, are those who sacrificed their appearances of being good, reasonable, or even sane so that we all didn't have to do so. Adamite is for those who are blaming themselves and or others.

Agate

Agate is the guardian angel essence, a first-aid and rescue remedy.

"When in doubt....take your agate out!" Anytime you are less than happy, healthy and high, we use agate until specifics are known or a more precise application is obtained.

Agate is a multi-colored, frequently striped or banded chalcedony. The name agate came from an ancient river called Achates on the island of Sicily. This river was a site purported to have held much agate.

As it is your first-aid, agate should always be close at hand. It is nice that agate is so very inexpensive and readily available. Any and all types of agate are, and can be used as, all-purpose first-aid when held in one's hand. As with most of the stones, it can be used also as an essence. (Carnelian is the only exception. See index)

In any given time of trauma, whether physical, emotional or spiritual, agate will sustain your being and nurture to wellness, everything from headache to heartache. Although each stone has a specific use and application, agate is the stone of choice for general assistance in any given situation. It is not by mere chance that so many "luck" items, like worry stones and worry beads were made from this family of chalcedony.

An additional quality of agate's vibrational influence is its value and importance when one is working to overcome an addiction or habit. (More so in self-abuse and indulgence areas of chemicals and tobacco than with chronic mental or emotional behavior patterns.) Agate is essential to the well being of both young and old

Alexandrite

Alexandrite is to assist men with their difficulties in adapting to the changes from a patriarchal to a matriarchal system.

This stone was named after Czar Alexander II. Alexandrite is a chrysoberyl, a rather rare stone, and very much needed at present. One means of obtaining its influence is by locating a stone and rendering its essence, though not purchasing the stone. This should be taken by all men four times a day, four drops at a time, for seven to ten days in order to become acclimated to the role of women in this new age. This influence is seen as an induction to enlightenment, rather than therapy for a recurring malady. This application of help is not to be confused with or replaced by periodot for enlightened discernment, or petrified wood for emotional balance. This is a precise directive of harmony and balance, of strong, dominating male qualities and feminine attributes of equality in service and contribution.

Some men are demonstrating many of the gentler aspects of matriarchal guidelines, such as parenting and home-keeping. These pioneer spirits will have a much easier transition than the proverbial "Archie Bunker" types. Alexandrite is to aid in the change of states of awareness to a joyful acceptance of the value of nurture and care for each other.

This is a brother being his brother and sisters' keeper.

Amazonite

Amazonite is the judgment stone.

It is to eliminate judgmental attitudes in us towards others, and in others toward us, and to breed good judgment. Amazonite came of age on August 16, 1987, which was Judgment day. Such is the way of the spirit to have brought about these changes of ages in manners that would herald comfortably and soothingly the awakening of humankind to their heaven here on this mother earth.

Amazonite will remove attitudes of judgment regarding one's brethren's manner, custom, appearance, practices and beliefs. Most importantly, Amazonite sets the value judgment center in balance while educating the conscious mind in the utilization of good judgment with good judgment.

The storied celebration of this stone is the judgment itself. The creator contracted with us millennia ago, predisposing a future visit of the light of the spirit. As it passed near, it turned its face toward Earth hoping to see 144,000 souls still glorifying creation. On that day of Harmonic Convergence, August 16, 1987, we showed closer to 144 million of us looking for the love light! Of course we outdid ourselves. How could we not, since we are all part and one with this great creation? As we see by these gifts and tools of enlightenment, our judgment went in full favor of harmony, peace and love. We've already won. We are safe, saved and secure.

In our well recorded history we have the guarantee of this new age. Humankind's abilities have taken hatred and lies to a state of art. Nazi Germany and the threat of nuclear annihilation are two good examples. When we've applied our new knowledge of the mineral kingdom to the daily task of wellness for ourselves and our environment, we will exist in a state conducive to the entrance of the Divine Presence (in a state of readiness). At the moment, the only thing this space is ready for is help. In a state of well-being, it is guaranteed that you will not find any two or three together in any name but Love.

Amazonite begins a precious course of healing for us all. Rock-Medicine is a total format of vibrational balancing. Applying the principles of good judgment to the physical and mental bodies has as full a myriad of potential as the previously described spiritual aspects.

Amazonite is particularly well-sistered with aventurine, which is the stone for prejudice.

Amber

Amber is the memory stone, and for proper DNA structure.

Amber is a fossilized form of pine resin. It is one of the oldest crystal formations on the planet. Amber is essential to any application of Rock-Medicine, as it carries the memory to the area afflicted of what that area's proper state of wellness is. You can see where this quality would be most applicable in extreme cases especially, such as multiple sclerosis, Alzheimer's, and muscular dystrophy. Amber is one of the stones indicated to use for ALL physical maladies.

Amber uses your own DNA to lock on to a previously well state whether it be your own or, in the case of one being born with an imbalance, the well state of an ancestor.

Being the memory stone, it is quite literally applied to anyone whose memory is ailing. Effective uses may be for recalling specific instances in this lifetime, or for past life recall. Amber is not, however, the stone for past-life regression. That stone is talc.

Just as a single cell of our body carries the full equation as to our being, so it is with the stones themselves. One small chip or fragment of any stone is just as effective as is a huge boulder-sized one. Each one of the stone's cells carries the full vibration of that stone's influence. As long as it is a true representative of its particular mineral family, your Rock-Medicine instruments can be any size. It is more a question of practicality as to what rocks each household acquires.

Memory of wellness is equally applied to the physical broken leg as it is to the mental and spiritual attributes which allowed the break in the first place. Remembering ancient Egypt, we see the presence of great amounts of amber. The Atlantians took stone-healing principles to Egypt, among other places. Also, they took to the Egyptians the higher-level techniques of vibrational power-wielding, such as telekinesis and levitation. Isis is one of the most well remembered Atlantians. Her job was -- and still is -- to teach humankind to heal.

Inspiration is the conscious memory of the future.

Amethyst

Amethyst is for cell division and for alcohol detoxification.

Amethyst comes from the Greeks, literally meaning "not intoxicated" or not toxic. This has been and remains an influence of this stone's vibration. When drinking alcohol, if an amethyst is placed in the glass or bottle, its energy negates the physically toxic poisons. This means you get the same altered state of consciousness, but no headache, nausea or hangover, no matter how much is drunk. Either a real amethyst gem or quartz may be used here. However, there is a grave area of caution: If one has a problem with alcoholism, such as blackouts, rages depression or dependency, this is an addiction, and must first be addressed as such.

The sages of old used wine for altering their states of consciousness, just as we use drugs and exercises to alter ours. Herein was the knowledge of the gift of the holy grail to men by celestial beings. They used the expanded state of mind to create ideas and the teaching of those ideas. The danger that alcohol poses is its toxicity. Anything used to excess is toxic (Don't worry, though, there is no such thing as an excess of love, as nothing exceeds it!)

As an application for cell mitosis (or cell division), this means that anywhere there is a disruption of the cell structure, amethyst is used. Whether it be a broken bone, tumorous growth, tissue breakdown or even acne amethyst will be the catalyst for cell movement. Amethyst should never be used alone. It is as a soldier with blinders on to all but it's job to cause cells to divide. It makes no distinction on its' own between well and ill cell structures. It receives its' direction from the stones you add to it. Amethyst should not be worn alone as its' nature will serve to cause more severe results at times of burns, cuts and all other types of injury.

In the case of burns the burnt portion should be covered in honey. Honey aborts the burning process. Next, it immediately addresses the pain. It ensures an infection-free wound and minimizes the scar tissue. (As healing progresses, aloe vera may be alternated with honey as treatment.)

In a situation such as cancer, where the action is mutating cells, amethyst serves to perpetuate the mutation. Using calcite, which is anticancer, with the amethyst, changes the polarity of its influence by combining it with another stone.

Amethyst is also an excellent influence to have in procedures and techniques surrounding infertility.

Amethyst can be administered to one intoxicated by alcohol for detoxification when combined with jade, smokey quartz, hematite and lepidolite. The benefits of this stone are limitless. Amethyst quartz in its rough mineral state is inexpensive and readily available, although gem quality amethyst works equally well.

All minerals work to their highest potential when in their most natural state.

Apatite

Apatite is for proper metabolizing of nutrients.

This stone is a very good example of how simple this work truly is. This rainbow-lustered crystal is named just about what it addresses. Any weight or food allergy problem should be treated with apatite. All weight imbalance situations need the metabolism balanced whether it be obesity or anorexia. This element of proper digestion of food can be clearly typified in the old adage "You are what you eat." Just think a moment about the mental and spiritual correlation to the obvious physical ones.

Our beautiful mother Earth has provided us with a vast array of nutritional staples. It is a common fallacy among the metaphysical community that any member of the animal kingdom are off limits as a foodstuff. This is as ludicrous an assumption as that of the mineral kingdom not having consciously controlled powers of cause and effect. All that exists is made up of light energy. This includes all elements of the animal, vegetable and mineral kingdoms. Being of the same light energy, yet vibrating at individual rates of speed to produce individuality, all things, therefore, carry within themselves the full spectrum of light color bands. This correlation between the kingdoms of life forms is what enables us to utilize herbs, for example, to address a malady. Now, however, there is a toxic level of impurities, both from airborne pollutants and radiation, and soil and water pollutants as well. It is virtually impossible to obtain untainted food or herbs unless they are raised hydroponically with purified water and in a sterile atmosphere. This is not by any means cost-effective or practical at this point in time. Nor is it necessary since we now have these new instruments helping us with the clean-up of ourselves and the environment. You cannot treat something toxic with something toxic and get anything other than something equally toxic.

All that we take in on every level becomes some part of our being. A good example of how this equates to the consumption of meat products is whenever you ingest or partake of anything you are making its qualities one with yours. In the case of venison, the deer is a gentle and beautifully spirited animal. The offer of thanks before a meal is the conscious acknowledgment of the sacrifice of what is about to be received, and from whence it came. Then it can be with celebration and appreciation that we can accept all that has been provided to meet our every need.

Because we are all the same energy, there are correlating bands of intensity that match a member in each kingdom of mineral, vegetable, and animal. When we find the matches, so to speak, we can use the influence of one in order to tune or balance another. This is the principle upon which all things work to elicit harmony or well-being.

Aquamarine

Aquamarine is for the toothache, infection, inflammation or damage of tooth and/or gums. Ultimately it denotes the mouth.

The name aquamarine is derived from Latin and means "water of the sea". The application of this stone in combination with others signifies that the area of illness is located in the mouth. Combining aquamarine with coral and the seven cleansers specifies treatment of the teeth and jaw bone. Aquamarine with rhodocrosite and the seven cleansers treats the gums and other tissue in the mouth. It will serve to eliminate inflammation, infection and pain as well as help with more serious conditions until a dental practitioner can be seen. An essence can be applied topically, directly on the area, such as in the case of a teething baby.

These instruments are not to throw aside the conventional medical practices as a whole. They work in conjunction with them. There are, however, many means of chemical and physical therapy which have toxic residuals and side effects. These will be replaced by Rock-Medicine. Although there are several safeguards and cautions to Rock-Medicine, they are standardized and easily observable.

As the function of the teeth and gums is to process food intake for distribution into the system, so is it for the mental and spiritual aspects of processing input.

A broken tooth, injured gum or root decay are problems that require some physical assistance. Just as if in the event one breaks their leg, obvious action must be taken as well as applying the appropriate stones for pain, cell mitosis and emotional balance.

Aragonite

Aragonite is for unity (between man and woman, their sisters and brothers and all cosmic nature).

Aragonite is crystallized deposits of hot springs calcium carbonate. This stone is for unity and all that it represents. It is especially suited for disputes between friends, business associates, fellow students or workers, club or church members, anywhere that a group or community formed as a body finds dissent. (For the application of this same kindred ship between family and members you would use ulexite. Aragonite may be added also). This mineral is best known for its appearance as stalactites and stalagmites in Carlsbad Cavern.

A less well known occurrence of major proportions is in Nevada on the Pyramid Lake Paiute Indian Reservation. The Pyramid Lake area is made up of vast deposits of this mineral. It is no wonder then that this was the site of a musical event held specifically to send out a vibrational spiral of unity and healing. This event was called "Ranch Rock". One of the miraculous results of that show was the preservation of the rights of the Paiutes to their water. Some of the earliest prophecies concerning the rainbow tribe (a united humankind) have come out of the Paiute teachings. On September 7, 1986, the gathering there joined in dance, prayer and song. It became the germination process of a collective of seeds carried among many hearts.

This stone represents an intensifying of a world unity. Nowhere more than in the concept of unity do we see the potential for the success of a vibrational spiral of positive energy. The Yin must always be, and so must the Yang. Fortunately for us, there is the interplay of the karmic equation. This principle enables us to experience the negativity and arrive at an attainable point of "done" with the manifestation of its presence. Only after this occurrence does the guarantee come into existence of our lessons from the past, ensuring a bright future.

Aragonite unites our spirits individually and collectively, as well as the mental capacities and physical interactions (the only exception is the uniting one with the higher consciousness, which is the work of diamond).

Aventurine

Aventurine is to eliminate prejudice of any kind.

This glossy green stone was named in the 17th century after a green Italian glass known as aventura which it resembled. As mentioned earlier by the author, this stone is a companion stone to amazonite which is for judgments. Aventurine addresses all forms of prejudice. This includes the obvious aspects such as race, creed or religion. It is also applicable for countering prejudicial attitudes regarding sexual preferences, attire, mannerisms, handicaps and behaviors. Prejudice is admittedly amongst the most destructive of all human made forces. This harsh medium is most often perpetuated by an ongoing process of actual education. Parents teach their young by example and direct suggestion. The same format occurs anywhere groups are educated in churches, schools, social clubs, media perception and governmental organizations. As we have said before, the swing towards the light has already taken place. Thoughts of prejudice of all kinds are recognized as obstructive to peace.

Aventurine may be used for your own feelings of prejudice, to disrupt gatherings of energies that would methodically participate in prejudicial thoughts, words or deeds. It gives radical strength to all anti-prejudice activity. We must be very careful as the tones around us and of us resonate higher. Our job is to shed light by example. Knowledge is a moot issue until its proper application transforms it into wisdom. It has oft been said "The wise man has the power". Wisdom is the discretion and tact with which we take the knowledge into our responsibility and act according to that which nurtures and perpetuates positive growth of all creation.

Changes for this can only occur now in this new age as they do in nature in a flow of adaptation of the evolutionary process and in a kind and considerate manner towards our oneness. This state requires enlightenment or conscious awakening of the spirit as a catalyst.

Azurite

Azurite promotes "self-heal" and can be used to enhance the usage of time spent in "dreamstate".

This brilliant blue stone gets its name from its azure-blue color. When you see a particularly well crystallized example it is almost possible to see the universe it its glimmer. Azurite is a most precious stone in that it facilitates the self-heal process. This is invaluable when the nature of the malady eludes one. Using the stone or its essence sends the unconscious mind on a seeking mission as it were. It travels throughout the entities body and spirit, combines the input with its own information and begins the areas healing even before a diagnosis is reached.

You may be asking then "Why not just use azurite for every ailment?" Azurite has been provided in the event the truth about the infirmity is unknown. Obviously, you would elicit much more expedient healing were you to use a stone that specifically and with precision tunes the correlating band of vibration inherent to the affected area.

When azurite is used to work in dream state, the application is for the stone to be held on the forehead or third eye for 10 to 15 minutes right before going to sleep. Do not secure it there and try to sleep. It is a disquieting saturation when over-applied. This means of obtaining first person presence in your sleep state is one that allows you to consciously continue your self-improvement process on the mental and spiritual levels while the physical body is resting.

It is advisable to take a break from a daily routine of use at least one night a week. A good choice might be the day you choose to take as your Sabbath. The day of rest is essential to every individual's life. It is absurd to think that the creator had need of rest and we need not. Especially now at this birthing and beginning of a new world.

Azurite is quite often found growing jointly with malachite. Azurite is one tool unto itself, malachite another and the combination of the two form yet a third. The combination rock azurite/malachite is for paranoid schizophrenia. This condition is at epidemic proportions world-wide at present.

Azurite/Malachite

Azurite/Malachite is for paranoid schizophrenia.

This disease is one of the front-runners for the most prominent epidemic planet-wide. This is not surprising as we learn that radiation toxicity affects us human beings in the thyroid gland. The thyroid gland is the seat of inspiration and anxiety. When thyroid toxicity goes untreated by covellite, the resulting illness is this condition known as paranoia and paranoid schizophrenia. At this advanced stage, covellite alone is not effective, and thus the introduction of azurite/malachite.

The application is either by holding or essence and can take anywhere from 10 days to 8 weeks to be alleviated depending upon severity. You may still use the combination stone as either a malachite or azurite depending upon which is of greater physical presence. The best results however do come from a pure form of one or the other.

When we look at the individual influences of these two elements which almost exclusively grow together, we can see how they combine their qualities for use here. Azurite promotes self-healing. Without the ability for the mind to perceive a state of wellness, azurite works to independently reorganize the thought processes for the return of mental clarity. Malachite brings focus of vision. As the azurite is balancing perception of reality, the malachite centers the mind's eye on a conscious focus of that reality and thus enables one to return to mental stability.

In order to prevent the return of the advanced toxicity, a continued application of covellite is required until such a time as the radiation levels return to a natural and safe level in the environment. Covellite is needed by all things living at this point in time, and azurite/malachite is highly advisable for use as a preventive measure by all humans.

The ability to manifest creative desire is the single-most valuable prerequisite for the promotion of a healthy existence on this planet.

Barite

Barite is for fungi. Moldavite is for molds. The use of both of these together is advised when treating such situations as ringworm, candida, yeast infections, etc.

Remember to include all pertinent information while forming your Rock-Medicine sentence. The barite and moldavite will be directed to the involved area(s). In the example of ringworm, you would then go on to include rhodocrosite which says: "epidermal tissue, surface and exterior". Next your basics jade, amber, covellite, hematite (or carnelian depending on the age), smokey quartz, clay and pyrite. These are the cleansers of toxicity blockage, DNA, thyroid, blood, water content, immune system and air in the lung space. Add amethyst for the motion of cell division and for this single condition you have a complete prescription.

Beryl

Beryl is to awaken the psyche to its skills and education. (i.e.: psychic awareness, abilities such as telepathy foresight, out of body, etc.)

Beryl is any member of the "precious beryl" family not being aquamarine or emerald. Most frequently seen around local lapidary shops is the green and yellow. Red is rare but all beryls work as well no matter what the color. This was one of the primary occurrences at the harmonic convergence. The vibrational family bands converged with harmony towards each other and as a result jade is jade is jade no matter the color, agate is agate is agate, no matter the type. So it is with all mineral families. There are a few variations on this theme but they are well indicated in the text.

Good judgment is called for when entering the higher level work stones. It is imperative that any growth process have a state of well being as its base. Always address obvious and necessary relief from illness, whether it be poor vision, allergies or any physical imbalance, before venturing on in your course of study. Although we already envision the true potentials before us, as is typified in new age art and music, we must follow a strategic guideline and design. Out of body experiences are but primary exercises predisposed to make the ways of teleportation astral travel, time travel and the like obtainable. Before such an advanced culture can exist, however, there is a lot of work, cooperation and organization necessary to afford the higher consciousness' help with the practical and technological, as well as medical needs of this particular plane of existence.

The psychic abilities are a source of delight in higher education. Education remains the same on every level in its potential for either progress, or through unapplied or misapplied practices, for digression. We stand the same propensities towards our performance being rewarded an "A" to an "F", depending upon our dedication, whether it be the physical world or a higher level of existence.

Bloodstone

Bloodstone is for the HIV virus.

AIDS is not a "sexual" disease. Having AIDS means having the HIV virus in the bloodstream and the measure of ones "T" cells being below 200. The attack upon the immune system and resultant breakdown of natural defenses opens one up or makes one vulnerable to virtually all invasive infections. Bloodstone is specifically for the elimination of the HIV presence from the bloodstream at the pre-AIDS stage. As with other diseases treated by Rock-Medicine, this application is to heal the condition present and not to merely maintain or sustain one at the level of a given illness's progress. The combination of jade, amber, bloodstone (heliotrope), clay, hematite, pyrite, covellite and smokey quartz is for elimination of the HIV-presence in approximately 6-8 weeks. However, if there are other conditions present such as brain infection and/or lesions, tumors, abrasions, etc., these must all be treated with additional combinations of stones per their specific nature as well as the administration of the AIDS essences or stones.

With the extreme fear factors concerning the AIDS syndrome, it is advisable that careful consideration be made with regard to the use of additional stones such as petrified wood for emotional balance and aventurine for prejudicial attitudes of others. The use of the combination of stones for AIDS can also be used preventively by those close to and/or working with AIDS victims.

Of course, as with all illnesses, it is most beneficial to treat the afflicted with the utmost of love, kindness, and regard for their dignity. Nowhere more than in dealing with this deadly disease has this issue been looked at. We should always remember this lesson in caring for that which is not well of body, mind, or spirit.

Bornite

Bornite is the stone for arrogance. It is one of three which combine for male hormone balance.

Bornite is a metallic rainbow lustered rock. Its slang name is "peacock ore". It is the first stone we come to that is a hormone balancer for men. In combination with ulexite and citrine it brings the full male hormonal fabric into balance on the physical, emotional and spiritual bodies. All individuals have male and female hormones, but rarely if ever, will a woman require so strong an application as this triad. Certain single aspects of the three will certainly apply at times. No matter what sex you refer to your self as being, it is your biological chromosomal origin that determines your use of male triad vs. female triad.

This glittery stone does away with unnecessary and even dangerous trappings. Self righteous attitudes, arrogance, pride these are qualities which contributed to the format system know as patriarchal.

The opposition of patriarchal to matriarchal is not necessarily consistent with male-female relationships, but rather, the relativity of an individual's perception of the best of both those qualities within themselves. We are definitely not lacking in the past examples at all extremes of classically female duty and behavior as well as male. In no area can we better see the contrast of the beauty and potential ugliness derived out of over-bearing vs. bearing up one another of control and command of other than oneself vs. self-discipline. Another way of putting these comparisons is the masculine-patriarchal leaderships of forces that have resulted in death and destruction of the human spirit.

Rising out of that change is its natural flow of counterpart or polar opposite which is the feminine-matriarchal tendency towards home keeping and fostering young. This quality is a partner to fidelity. Fidelity means faithful, loyal, and true. We received an analogy to this concept in the fable of the ugly duckling who survived due to the mothering instinct.

Calcite

Calcite is for cancer. (There are some specifics pertaining to color). Calcite may be used as a preventative measure where the attitude held by one indicates a predisposition to manifesting this disease of attitude. Take severe introverts, for example, whose attempts to suppress create blockages that fester and grow awry or malignantly due to their freedom being denied, or take a simpler example in the results on the spirit of a wild animal when caged. The direct use of calcite on cancer is as follows:

White calcite is the general application stone for cancer anywhere in the body and in most forms. White is also the stone of choice for treatment of the side effects of chemo-radiation therapy the dizziness, nausea, exhaustion and weakness brought on by the residuals of that energy. (When treating this chemo-radiation sickness combine the white calcite with cobalt).

The condition cancer is a stranger to no area of our body. Therefore, as you treat in general the causes, you need to pay particular attention to the availability of information pertinent to the specific body part(s) involved. (i.e. Herkimer diamond's affect on the throat, larynx, vocal chords and voice box).

Pink calcite is most specifically for leukemia. It is applicable to sickle-cell anemia also. Ultimately we shall locate a pink calcite chamber in the mountains of Tibet wherein many similarly evolved blood disorders will be speedily cured. Remember that leukemia is a form of cancer and the blood must be treated with hematite as well as the underlying emotional perceptions being evaluated and addressed (or the causes in attitude).

Yellow calcite is for most lower extremity level organs afflicted, such as kidney, liver, pancreas, bladder, and uterine and vaginal cancers.

Green calcite is applied when the areas afflicted are in the spleen, colon, intestines or digestive tract.

Blue calcite is indicated for use where the lymph or glandular system is infected with the cancer.

Benign tumors, except for brain tumors, may be treated with calcite but the results will be discretionary based upon the true causes. This includes external as well as internal abnormal tissue growth, or skin eruptions.

Carnelian

Carnelian is for use by those over 55 as a blood purifier, strengthener, and enhancer.

It is named for its color resembling that of a type of cherry known as Kornel. The reason there is a specification regarding the age of the one treated is because of the bridge between the generations. The antiquity of the evolution of the generation preceding the current middle age group uses an influence resonating at a slightly different rate than the hemostructure of the next generation. (The stone of choice for blood purification by the generation under 55 is hematite). Therefore the carnelian replaces it or, if in doubt, is added to the seven cleanser grouping. The application can be either by hand or by essence in a four-times a day standard of application. This would apply to most, but not all, blood related maladies.

As it is the function of the heart organ to process and distribute the blood throughout one's system it is always wise to treat the heart with cinnabar, especially in geriatrics who are having blood disorders. Since the three bodies of physical, mental and spiritual are joined as they are, enhancement of performance of the blood itself, and all such flows, can be addressed by these stones (maladies such as high or low blood pressure will be relieved, using garnet in combination as well).

Celestite

Celestite is for truth.

All perceived aspects regarding truth are most expeditiously administered to with celestite. Whether it be the truth about a situation or your ability to handle a given truth, indeed, even the fortitude to elicit the truth its presence serves as a reminder of the importance of truth to all existence, especially considering the fact that we progress by way of adaptation and, if unnatural/ untrue energies do too much damage, we could have irretrievable opportunities.

There exists no situation in which lies are better than the truth, but there is a valid amount of truth that hurts. This is sometimes unavoidable. An abuse or incorrect use of the truth is when the intended result is to hurt another. Celestite is better suited for states of denial than any other stone, especially regarding addictions and attitude or behavior problems. The sociopath denies his relationship to his world around him and would therefore also be treated with celestite. (If the source of his pathological behavior is found to be organic add lepidolite for brain chemical balance.)

An ancient legend (as told by Chapman) typifies for us the value in the naked truth. Truth and Falsehood once went bathing. When they came out of the water, Falsehood ran ahead, dressed herself in Truth's clothing and ran away. Truth, unwilling to appear in Falsehood's clothing, went "naked". It is no wonder the most heinous of personages conceptualized by mankind is the satanic "Father of Lies". All evil is represented by the absence of the light of truth.

Knowing the absolutes of our existence better equips us to take a more total control of ourselves in and of our environment. The application as pertaining to the use of this stone in treatment of lying is that where chronic and habitual lying is the case and the presence of delusion. (This does not include artificially stimulated states of delusion.) Lies are love's polar opposite. Without the benefit of having truth as your grounding, it is impossible to exist any further beyond the state of being earthbound.

Chalcedony

Chalcedony is a shield system.

The Chalcedony family is a large group which includes the agates, chrysoprase, heliotrope, fossilized wood, jasper, carnelian, onyx and sand.

As you continue through this text note the variations on the precise applications of like or related minerals. We shall incorporate the individual stones in the previously used manner of alphabetized order bearing in mind that this is a mineral family with many similarities in appearance thus the common reference to them as chalcedony for their structural generalizations. Different stones provide different types of protection or shielding. Some of these differences are very subtle, such as in the case of jasper and onyx.

Chrysocolla

Chrysocolla is for the comprehension, recall, retention and application of one's education. It is the matriarchal stone.

This vibrantly blue-green beauty is a queen among stones. She is the manifestation of wisdom. Education is being conscious. We are all educating ourselves, by every working sense, throughout our lives. A once respected thing to have was an alma mater. This term indicating a college education was coined from the Latin phrase literally meaning "nursing", or nourishing mother. The indication is that a nourished or nurtured mind is instinctive to survival, more so even growth.

The earliest thought processing periods in one's life are the most important by virtue of their edge on longevity. The longer information is stored in the brain the more refined its virtues become understood by the conscious and sub-conscious repetition of those resources. This exemplifies the matriarchal quality of the value placed on a baby by its mother and indeed those other women in its life. The younger the more pure and vulnerable. So is it with this new age of ours we must nurture this new enlightened state of being into growth, health and celebration.

Chrysocolla is ideal for the academic pursuits. Use by holding the stone in the appropriate hand while studying, reading, attending lecture/class or while testing. This applies to any type of formal learning situations, whether it be on the physical, mental or spiritual level.

Both the sub-conscious mind and conscious minds are conscious. It is their utilitarian interaction with the whole that puts the level of quality and success to our education of consciousness (or the demonstrative results). Higher education is the demonstrative result of the sharing of wisdom or a cooperative effort with regard to knowledge. Knowledge is a means to obtaining wisdom and wisdom must precede education. We understand the concept of incorrect by way of our current educational system. Everything has an ultimate potential for life or destruction or good and bad. Wrong and its ramifications are always realistic potentials but so are the same degrees of potential for love. In this world of third dimensional barriers we have received the tools and the education to improve the quality of all existence on a conscious level. These gifts were wrought from our own world's collected conscious and sub-conscious creative desire. We manifested our own destiny...to be enlightened.

When using chrysocolla for the higher studies it works particularly well when joined with silver, as this combination causes the vortex of energy to be directed at the highest chakral point, which is at the highest point of your aura. (Since the harmonic convergence, our transformation caused us to be aware of every cell in our body as the chakra it now is. This gives us the fundamentals of the keen awareness required for self-control).

Where knowledge, or truth, is present with self-discipline, or proper education, there in their midst is unconditional love.

Chrysoprase

Chrysoprase is for pain.

This translucent, apple to bluish-green stone is much needed for its influences in addressing the despair of pain. Pain weighs heavy on the mind, body and soul. It always takes obvious tolls on one's life.

When addressing physical pain from injury, surgery or strain, the most effective application is to hold it in the appropriate hand as needed. Now if the pain is served in its purpose to indicate to the being the presence of damage, then you are well to treat the pain. If, however, the signal of pain has not been diagnosed then it is still a needed source of input. Chrysoprase is the best known treatment for relief from pain, which makes one more receptive to treatment of the source.

Emotional pain is on parallel course with the physical and spiritual. The height of pain is seen on the face of the creator and can only be likened unto the most agonizing of loss over a loved one. Take the extreme you've known in any given moment of true breakage of heart or spirit and know that HE has felt this, and more, since we have been away from each other for these millennia. The divine presence is as ready as we are for heaven on earth.

The most assured way to do away with pain and sickness is to decide to. That is the act of faith. Proclaiming so by way of example and opinion is the act of commitment. Semantics has never come more into play than in these times of mass communication. The term "decide" comes from Latin and means "cutting away". Decidere - arriving at a decision by eliminating all but one possibility, by cutting away all that is worthless (Chapman). In this time of awakening to the presence of a higher consciousness, let's not be so concerned as to which of His infinite names we call Him, but that we all do call upon the availabilities of the benefits of His unconditional love in our individual and united daily lives. We were conceived of love and light and our potential for growth flourishes nowhere better than under those conditions which love promotes. This same love, a conscious thought, put a healing vibrational instrument inside solid rock, safe and within hands reach to await its coming of age. We always have been safe in the rock of ages. That the desire for love to lead us is again mankind's desire is well represented by the way this world is making known its desire for peace. It has evolved to conscious action and has won us the opportunity to choose eternity. Chrysoprase allows us to choose to be without pain.

For cases of long term, chronic physical pain, you would do well to use an essence and saturation level to elicit complete relief over a period of some 3-4 weeks bearing in mind always that whenever a standard of application does not work, you are using the wrong one. Re-evaluate.

Cinnabar

Cinnabar is for the strength of the heart organ and its valve function.

Cinnabar is extremely mercury-toxic. Mercury poisoning could result if handled too much or if it were to be ingested. So, obviously you would not make an essence out of it or hand hold it. The safe way to use your cinnabar is to keep a clear quartz crystal stored with it, thus setting the crystal to "be" cinnabar. The quartz, once wiped clean of any cinnabar dust, may safely be used in any of the applications.

Cinnabar no doubt got its name from its own beautifully rich cinnamon color. This ancient Chinese favorite is not easily come by, as it is rare and expensive. Our hearts carry the life force in all definitions of that term. Man has seen through the lion's den of hell by virtue of his conviction of heart. The heart has been the keeper of the lovelight and its progress. The ancient Greeks coined the term "to learn something by heart" based upon their belief that the heart was the seat of thought. As we see by the timely reinstatement of the mineral kingdom's vibrational tools, even a stone, especially each stone, has conscious placement in service of value. So, take heart, all hearts of stone can be softened.

The parallel conditions existing in the emotional and spiritual aspects of the heart coincide. Romantic interaction is the exception to the use of this stone of the heart. See the guidelines of ruby. At the harmonic convergence, the seat of thought moved, evolved and transitioned upwards, to relocate itself in its new anatomical position atop the aura. Do not confuse the function of the heart of venting a portion of the grief process, with its capacity for acting as the agent of awareness. In the first function, that of the fundamental acknowledgment of a loss, the ensuing distresses are healed with rose quartz. As the guide energy, however, the keeper of trust, or the truth chords' ability to consciously confirm our understandings, we apply cinnabar. Note that heart damage and scar tissue, or the equivalent of, is a presence on each of the three bodies. Think carefully before causing damage to another's heart, as you take, each time in doing so, an element of wholeness from yourself. Cinnabar is also invaluable for pre and post heart surgery.

Citrine

Citrine is for irritability it is one of the triad for male hormone balance and is for itch.

There is more than we have now to know about this stone. The golden sun yellow of this stone serves to remind us of its virtues. Citrine is one of the three stones for male hormone balance the other two are ulexite and bornite. Citrine combines with the other two for bringing harmony to the male hormone balance system. As stated with bornite, women will never use the combination of the three. They will, however, find use of them for their individual applications. Citrine relieves irritability, manic behavior, and the inability to organize and tend to our intrapersonal relationship with our environment. It is for energies which are scattered and working at odds towards each other, and for counter productive or self-destructive tendencies. These are all strong patriarchal characteristics.

We find that citrine is particularly soothing to skin irritations, but just of the itch itself, and not the physical presence of rash or outbreak. The presence of both sensory manifestations is redundant, and so, welcome relief from the itch while working on diagnosing the condition. This is applicable for allergic reactions, fungi and all surface area, non-invasive diseases.

Clay

Clay is for detoxification of the cell structure of the immune system.

When we speak of using clay as an instrument of Rock-Medicine, it is always in reference to a piece of pottery which is in excess of 400 years old. The reason for this is because of the porous texture of clay in its natural state. All of the surface and sub-surface clay has been affected or contaminated by air, soil, and water-born pollutants. Since the density factor of clay is so slight, it has absorbed all of the toxic elements over the course of time. If, however, you use a piece of clay pottery over 400 years old, you insure against getting an impure vibration. The ancient method of making pottery was to take clay and mix it with water. After a vessel or plate was fashioned, it was then sun-dried or fire-baked, and became hard, strengthening its density factor.

It then no longer was susceptible to the residual pollutants which have since been introduced. Luckily, man's recent penchant for preserving the past has afforded us vast collections of these pieces of pottery in museums and privately-held displays.

It is very interesting that the same clay which is applicable in the cure of the dreaded AIDS-virus is also the tool used to treat the common cold. Clay is used anywhere the immune system is adversely affected or out of balance. Some areas of use include allergic reactions as well as flu viruses. It is recommended that clay be included in all general and preventive-measure application of Rock-Medicine, due to the nature of the natural defense which is a healthy immune system.

Clay with smokey quartz is used for the purification of body fluids.

It seems quite appropriate that this element of healing is only available to the modern world, in a usable pure state, due to the development by our ancestors of utilitarian implements. In this, our past has contributed to the preservation of our future.

Coal

Coal is for self-esteem.

This world's vast array of bodies can take no better or worse care of us than we take of them. Volcanic "pipes" of coal bear diamonds. There could be no greater contrast than the brilliance of the light of diamonds being born of the pitch black. The studies regarding our basic understandings of the yin/yang principles are guiding us to the conscious applications of energy, gearing us towards an equal and opposite existence from that which has been so destructive to our world. Our history is our equal and opposite future as of the coming of the new age. Good self esteem puts you at one with yourself and all others in the light of loving. Self love can be described many ways self-discipleship, self-disciplined, self-sustaining. This is the heart of survival. Life. Self fulfillment is perpetual once the self love is applied in each individual, with conscious regard for the fact that the self he abides within is the same unto all that abides without. This is the understanding of the terms referring to mankind as "Rainbow Tribe" and "Family", of being "at One" and the "I Am".

The collective self esteem is on the rise. Some areas of particular emergency status are those of teenagers, minorities, most psychotic behaviors, when forgiving one's self some misdeed, suicidal tendencies, fear of being alone, taking responsibility for one's own feelings, or for anyone dealing with a severe trauma as a result of personal attack by another.

Clearly, we see this coal is as multi-faceted a "rock" as a healing instrument, as the diamond is one of sheer beauty.

Coral

Coral is for regenerative purifying and strengthening of bone.

Coral is the calcified skeleton left behind by the tiny polyps secreting calcite one of our many mineral gifts from the oceans of the world. It is exactly what its representation indicates for the bone and the skeletal structure. The marrow itself is treated with iolite. The combining of calcite and coral is the obvious choice for bone cancer. If you add iolite to them you have indicated that the marrow is involved, add emerald, which says back, and you have now described with your stone sentence the condition spinal meningitis. Coral can be applied to all bone disruptions, breaks and calcium deposit growth on the bone itself. Weak or brittle bones will be strengthened. This is an invaluable aid for the spectrum of bone problems suffered by the elderly (i.e. Osteoporosis). The skeletal structure of anything is its base of support. The mental aspects of correlation here would be of the same nature. This is a good essence to use on small infants to add the insurance of good physical, mental and spiritual support and their development. Also, coral is well applied to those diseases where the skeletal functions have either atrophied or are breaking down.

The skeleton and teeth are all the dead leave behind to finally turn to ash.

Covellite

Covellite is for radiation toxicity and the so affected thyroid.

Covellite is one of the most sophisticated tools in Rock-Medicine. We say this because the most advanced form of human-made toxicity is radiation. Our whole planet and its environment and atmosphere are all toxic with radiation from all the by-products we've released. As with all the other polluting agents of our world, there is no area, save the mineral kingdom, that is not at a saturation point of toxicity. Now, with the introduction of the usage of cobalt to clear that area, we may treat ourselves from the inside out, and from the outside in.

It is the author's recommendation, that as you begin on your individualized schedule for healing, you include cobalt near the top of the list of priority areas. Elimination of the toxic effects of the radiation in our soil, air, water, organic matter and animals, will then leave us with a clearer view of what illnesses are left to address.

Radiation attacks the thyroid gland in a human being. This is manifested in countless symptomatic conditions. The thyroid gland is the seat of inspiration in the human body. Anxiety is produced when the thyroid is ailing. This anxiety often goes undetected and undiagnosed because of our current population's proportion of the masses afflicted.

One of the residual side effects of the presence of thyroid toxicity often noted is a condition called goiter. This is when the patient's metabolism is involved. A very large number of the obese who suffer from goiter are properly diagnosed thyroid conditions. The treatment for goiter includes both the covellite for the thyroid and apatite for proper metabolism.

Everything, everywhere on this planet needs to be treated for radiation poisoning. We can detox our food as well as tainted medicinal herbs using this in a focus direct. We can also use the covellite to treat other rock instruments that may be toxic due to direct exposure to radiation. Stones do not clear themselves of radiation toxicity without the application of covellite, as they will of other toxins over a three to four hour cleansing period. We can likewise treat our atmosphere with a power spread, bodies of water with essence, and the soil with instruments called wands.

On January 6, 1987, the knowledge of the use of this stone came through to begin the healing of ourselves and to facilitate the purging necessary to make way and ready our heavenly inspired home.

Diamond

Diamond is for harmony and balance consciously with the higher consciousness.

The diamond was an important herald of the matriarchal guidelines for this new age. It can be no coincidence of woman's roles here and the female propensity and affinity towards diamonds. As they say, "Diamonds are a girl's best friend". As it turns out they are for everybody.

The very same moment that the first diamond came into its own perfection was the same moment in time that the first man became enlightened. Such is the precision of the correlation of our development with all that is. There are no accidents. The existence of life and its inherent growth and development is its own catalyst for being. I believe the old adage that "necessity is the mother of invention" duly applies here. We are here because we needed to be and we survive because we need to. We will likewise be made whole with our creation because in order for existence to continue, we need to.

Diamond is for perpetuating a constant state of what we have called in the past meditation. This is a state of being, at all times, in one hundred percent focus of all of your energies, and their changing relationships to those vibrational influences it comes in contact with. This is the application of the state of meditation becoming a state of being. This is clear predisposition to our own abilities to partake of the miracles of creation and of creating.

Diamond may be safely used with any stone and at any length of time. It happens to be one of the three stones everyone should have on themselves for use at all times. Of the three, topaz and diamond are both suitable for constant use (while keeping your agate pocketed for first aid).

When combining diamond with any stone, the diamond serves to enhance and amplify the stone's ability to heal. Diamond can be a very expensive stone to acquire. Remember that the instrument you use need only be a true representation of the vibration of its family there is no diminishment of healing virtue by way of size, color, clarity or origin.

Dinosaur Bone

Dinosaur Bone is for waste.

Waste in any form is treated by this bone. This includes waste of time, waste of energy, waste of resources, wasting words, wasted efforts the list goes on and on.

Even in cases where anorexic conditions persist, the "wasting away" of the individual on all three levels is treated.

On a planetary scale, when applied in spreads, it will assist all of the animal, vegetable and mineral extinction's in progress, and prevent future ones.

Emerald

Emerald is for any back injury, surgery or stress related imbalance.

Chronic back problems are predominant in our society worldwide. The causes themselves differ. Problems from injury may involve disk, muscle and, or vertebrae. When the problem is stress related and painful stress pockets are concentrated in the back you combine petrified wood with the emerald and the seven cleansers. If the problem is spinal chord injury you would combine the appropriate stones indicated as are indicated for use. Some of these may include sulfur for inflammation of connective joint tissue. Halite would be used where muscle elasticity has been eroded. This could be a result of atrophy from lack of movement given a long period of immobility including states of coma. Coral is used where the bone itself is involved or calcium deposits are present, and iolite would indicate marrow is effected.

Some neck injuries will certainly be treated with emerald where the imbalance is directly related to or involves the connection from the base of the skull to the spinal column. This may range from actual damaged vertebrae to pinched, bruised and severed nerves.

As the back is a fundamental base of structural support and a "meeting ground" for the physical body's nerves and energy flows, so it is with the correlation of this area to the mind and spirit. In this age of healing it is now widely accepted that all three of the elements body, mind and spirit, are inseparably inter-related. It stands to reason, therefore, that the presence of illness in any of the three equates to the same problem manifesting in the other two. Likewise, the presence of health and balance in any one indicates the wellness of its counterparts.

Fluorites

Fluorites are natural wands (the octahedorons).

Of the many types of fluorite, much like the variances in beryls and chalcedonies, we have many different instruments. The wands for common use are the little to large octahedral forms. Each fluorite represents an individual and complete wand. The use and application of these are the closest that we get at present to miracle power wielding of ethereal control.

Fluorite wands should not be displayed for sale in an accessible way for others to touch and handle them the reason for this being, that the means by which we set a wand of fluorite to perform a specific healing influence, is by creative desire. One merely has to take the new fluorite in their hand and predispose, by thought or word, what the specific need is that instrument will be used on. It is forevermore set to this vibratory level. The same fluorite can be used by others for the same area of malady, as the one within the person, whose tool it is. Now, all of the stones have a use and purpose. Some cross over in their ability to relate for healing any given similar situation. There is always an optimal application and this is always the desired one to use. It is much less effective to set a fluorite for cancer than to use the calcites provided to address that illness.

Fluorite wands are best applied to personal remedies such as smoking, nausea, headache, vertigo and other like phobias, motion sickness, indigestion, nail biting, etc. These are the only wands we are authorized to use at the present!!!

Fluorite (rough) is for fluid conditions in the lungs.

This form of fluorite is as the standardized stone use. It addresses those conditions resulting in excesses of fluids in the lungs. This applies to pleurisy and congestion from colds or flu, as well as the more dramatic threat of infection and bronchial conditions. The application here is essence or held. This stone is invaluable for prevention of either damage or chronic residuals in small children with severe congestion. Many smokers suffer from excesses of fluids in their lung space and need this helped. The air pollution levels in many regions are also predisposing people to lung pollution, and where this results in lung fluid, is also pertinent to this application. (See black tourmaline)

Galena

Galena is for balanced breathing while in a meditative state.

Brilliant silver in color and box like in appearance, galena is of precision focus. This stone sets the physical rhythm of breathing to facilitate a state most conducive to that of a center of calm. (All types of respiratory illnesses are treated with galena. This includes asthma, bronchitis, emphysema and hyperventilation caused by panic or extreme physical exertion.) This translates into the spiritual respect of peaceful flow. The mind paces itself to the rhythm allowing a constant resonating towards creative progress. Since we are fast transforming to acute stages of awareness on individual levels, this state of meditation becomes more and more a state of being. See this mineral as a tool for the transformation of the physically earth-bound self into that of your divine or light-being self. This particular aspect of humankind's transformation on a personal level is aided by the hemimorphite crystal.

Galena comes out of the heart of all that is beastly in the state of Nevada. This power seat of the infrastructure of the socioeconomic system in the United States includes all the manifestation of energies taken to their points of extreme or to abuse. Nevada represents the dash for greed the enslaving and minimizing of the virtuous value of women and minerals. The vast expanse of ground area seen barren was test bombed instead of nurtured by we who are the garden's tenders. Nevada set precedents for the wealthy's fare and the absolute failure of all others their very ruin through laws sanctioned by a governing organization this is self-serving to the point of reckless destruction.

The United States is still the pioneer of freedom. We are a special people because of coming together under the flag of devotion to unified freedom. Meditation is our most widely used practice by those students of enlightenment to date. It affords the freedom of mind, body and spirit unto itself and the interaction of all creation. This is flow. Meditation takes many forms all the arts are meditations: music, dance, song, creative writing, swimming, fishing, hobbies and crafts, prayers, mantras, ohms, ceremony, offerings, walks, indulgence for entertainment (as opposed to educational), altered states of consciousness, yoga, TM, exercise and aerobics, hypnosis and all other trance states. Doing work in the dreamstate is a very fine and practical meditation as we enter into new states of being.

Garnet

Garnet is a general enhancer for the blood, and balances blood pressure.

There is a wide range of minerals which come under the family of garnet, ranging in color from brilliant green to deep red The most common of which are of the deep red variety. This stone is particularly helpful when used with hematite for the condition of hemophilia. A general application of essence or by hand-held method will strengthen and fortify the blood. It is indicated for use in most situations where blood chemistry is out of balance.

The influence of garnet is very subtle and is not meant to be used alone, unless used in weekly or bi-monthly preventative maintenance, or as a regular program to nurture one's state of well-being (see hematite and carnelian).

Garnet is the stone of choice for both high and low blood pressure, balancing the rate of force throughout the body's blood course.

The life flow's pressure is equally problematic when the spiritual and mental rates of force are disrupted. This pace setting device can be applied to specifically address one's discomfort of body, mind or spirit as the universal flows accelerate.

Gold

Gold is for strength of any manifestation, especially physical.

Gold is for strength and survival of the energies best potential for growth. This is with a particularly positive vibration. It is no wonder that the early alchemists lost their "heads" over gold as a means of hoarding energy instead of using all of it, or rather the taking in of no more of any one influence than is called for by the situation, or as needed.

White and yellow gold are good settings for those shield stones one chooses to use at lengths of time so as to make it appropriate for wearing. Gold will strengthen the effect of not only the stone it is touching, but will work individually for the body's strength. The only safeguard you must take into consideration with gold is that the presence of banding (bracelets and necklaces), or piercing the skin with metals is going to have a blocking effect on the meridial flows. These occurrences are as erratic in nature as our propensity towards individuality. The discomfort caused by the blockage may be instantly relieved by taking the jewelry off for a period of no less than ten minutes. This is a good practice for fainting, dizziness, nausea, or any medical emergency or situation. The exception to this rule is during surgery itself. Gold is a most beneficial influence on the body for the vitals and levels of tolerance. How odd that during surgery it is one of modern medicine's standard practices to remove the patient's jewelry, usually even the gold wedding bands. This is in direct contradiction with practicality.

Granite

Granite promotes kindness and gentleness.

Granite represents the nature of St. Francis of Assisi the caring for small children and all animals. This is expanded by the use of granite to include all life-forms. We are in a very ominous age of vulnerability. The delicate fabric of balance in nature has been severely damaged by cruelty and thoughtlessness. It is the equal responsibility of us all to turn the tide.

Gentleness and kindness are feminine qualities, but are neither exemplified in the behavior of all women, nor absent from all men's. Granite smooths the rough and gruff tendency which have been bred from fear and the high degree of competition by humankind for survival. The solitude of struggle due to the lack of grace has resulted in a society where a kind and gentle nature has been near-suicide for those promoting it. We all need granite. Fortunately, since we are in the midst of sure redemption at this point, granite is indicated for use in only obvious and extreme cases. It seems reasonable to administer blanket applications to correctional facilities (both to the inmates and staff), as well as to most geriatric, mental health, and child-care operations.

Granite is again one of those influences which is safe and a good idea to include if there is the slightest doubt as to its being needed. This earth and its inhabitants can use all the gentleness and kindness we can muster!

Halite

Halite is for the retention of muscle and skin elasticity.

Halite is particularly valuable for use by massage therapists' clients to aid in the full retention of muscle and tissue elasticity. Since it is necessary for the client to be completely relaxed in order to receive optimum benefit from his treatment, the best application is either hand held or essence on a formal program, relative to the frequency of visits prior to, not during, a session.

Even better is to have a "mini-spread" right in the room where the massage is taking place (this set up is described in the chapter on applications).

All forms of physical therapy, chiropractics and sports massage are highly benefited by this influence. So, too, is any type of "patterning" or range of motion exercises for limbs in a state of atrophy. This stone is an excellent preventative measure for geriatrics and victims of degenerative muscle disease. Halite is another fine influence to use on newborn or small infants to give a good foundational vibration to their growing body.

Halite is excellent for use by athletes to minimize cramps, rigidity and protection against greater degrees of injury. This would apply also to those individuals who work very physically strenuous jobs. All types of gymnasts and dancers will find halite beneficial for enhancing their performance likewise, all individuals on personal programs of fitness inclusive of aerobics, running, jogging or calisthenics.

As a healing influence halite is a part of the combination of stones used to address muscular dystrophy and related syndromes. More often than not, where we find the need for sulfur, halite goes hand in hand.

Hematite

Hematite is a blood purifier of the new generation.

The name is derived from the Greek word for blood. This is exactly what it addresses. This stone is used to treat virtually all blood infections, mutations and disorders. From AIDS to mononucleosis, blood disorders are addressed by the essence or holding of hematite. This is a new age stone and it looks it! Hematite acts to cleanse and purify the structure of the blood in people under the age of 55 (in contrast to the use of carnelian by those over 55).

You will notice as you study and apply this Rock-Medicine, that like the pictures in the Tarot, a rock's countenance holds many clues as to its nature and consciousness. Notice particularly the light given off by those stones such as hematite, diamond, hemimorphite, and covellite. Their luster represent the beacon of being of most value and importance to mankind's development of this new age of enlightenment.

Hemimorphite

Hemimorphite is for transformation.

Transformation at the base level would be applied as part of the combination for dramatic weight loss or gain, or where dramatic tumor or .i.adhesion is present.

Transformation is equated to many changes on every level. When searching for spiritual transformations, always make sure you have addressed the obvious areas of your physical and mental needs first. On the broad considerations of this stone, like many, it could be readily applied in most situations.

Herkimer Diamond

Herkimer Diamond is for the throat, larynx, voice box, and vocal chords.

This stone works very well on all forms of strain, irritation and infection of the neck area, interior and exterior. With the proper combinations added, you can direct the "rock-sentence" to apply therapy to such conditions as whiplash, cough and irritation due to cold, flu or allergies, damaged or atrophied vocal chords and voice box from injury, surgery or coma. Excellent for orators and singers, and works with calcite on cancers in the neck and throat areas.

Consider the many applications on an aesthetic level when used with celestite for the "voice of truth", with lava for the "voice of authority" (perfect for school teachers), or with red rock for the "voice of the spirit", not to mention granite for a gentle and kind vocalization.

Iolite

Iolite is for bone marrow.

This is one of the most recent of stones we have received information about. It's use is indicated where the bone marrow is effected. This would include certain forms of cancer and calcite, among other stones, would be added. Some blood disorders are likewise concentrated in the marrow and the iolite works as a guide to direct healing to the bone marrow itself.

Ivory

Ivory is for infertility.

The factors contributing to conditions of infertility are numerous indeed. Whether the cause is physical, mental, or spiritual, is irrelevant to the use of ivory. However, the stones used in combination will vary per specifics. For example, amethyst and rhodocrosite are added in those instances where abnormal epidermal activity is a contributing factor, as is the case in plugged tubes. There are many emotional imbalances which sometimes result in infertility. These should be treated with the appropriate stone as well as with ivory.

Remember, Rock-Medicine works to heal by correcting vibrational activity in the three bodies. If a person wishes to become pregnant and is not successful in doing so, no matter what the given cause, ivory must be used in addition to other indicated treatments and procedures. This is because ivory's function is specifically to address the lack of a state of pregnancy regardless of its cause.

Jacinth/Hessonite Garnet

Jacinth/Hessonite Garnet is for creative visualization.

This can be likened to a mineral hallucinogenic, because of it's influence on a visionary level. It differs from the chemical or herbal applications in that there is no residue when dealing with vibration as the catalyst. As a result, there are no "bad trips". The creative visions produced are the product of pure mental clarity.

This stone's use is another example of an advanced level of study and development and is not meant for use before having addressed one's obvious and general imbalances first.

Hand held, in essence or in a focus direct, jacinth will enable you to fully experience the reality in the creative mode. This was one of the stones present in Aaron's breastplate described in the Old Testament.

Jade

Jade is for detoxification of saturation levels from chemical, emotional and spiritual residuals causing blockages, and thus illness.

The use of this stone goes back to ancient Egypt and China. It is known as the "side stone" or "hip stone" because of its healing properties on the kidneys. Its name, however, comes from the Spanish conquest of Central and South America where it was traditionally used for kidney ailments. Jade means hip. ("Yu", the Chinese word for hip was never widely accepted as this stone's name.)

As any illness denotes a blockage in the energy flow, Rock-Medicine uses jade in every symptomatic condition. It is the grandfather of the healing stones and the first of the seven cleansers. The myth and mystique surrounding this stone is one of many threads which prevented the disappearance of true stone healing down through the ages.

As with agate and other stones, the color of jade used and the quality are not factors in the use or application. Jade is jade is jade, no matter what as long as its chemical composition is in the jade family. Rough, uncut, and unpolished jade is difficult to find, so as with other similar situations, use what you have rather than not beginning the healing process at all.

There are various applications with jade other than the usual method of essence or hand held. One of these has to do with tension headaches. For this purpose, the influence seems to work more efficiently when the jade is applied to either side of the temples and/or the middle of the forehead, wherever the pain is felt most . Another variation of use is any time there is a noticeable degree of heat or fever present in the affected area. The patient would then apply the jade directly to the area for a period of twenty minutes. This kind of topical application seems to work well in many different instances for immediate relief from pain. A good example of this would be jade and halite or sulfur applied directly to the back. For relief from the pain of arthritis use jade with sulfur directly on the area. The jade will feel very hot from its absorption of toxicity and must be left to clear before being used for another application or essence or replaced in a spread. This clearing process takes approximately three hours.

Jade is also a very good stone to be used preventively.

There is a wide spectrum of activities and professions where individuals would do well to take to wearing jade as a part of their routine attire. Some examples are the mental health fields and most all high "burn out" related work (anywhere there is extensive use of chemical, emotional, or residual elements). Always, with any application of Rock-Medicine, be sure to note the stone or crystal of choice in addition to the jade. One such instance might be as with an x-ray technician who would want to use covellite for the presence of radiation and jade to negate toxic levels of radiation saturation. There are no applicable safeguards, except taking care to use a cleared stone and remove within the given twenty minute time frame.

Remember....jade is used for all .physical applications of Rock-Medicine.

Jasper

Jasper is a shield stone for positive outcomes.

Confrontation does not always mean conflict. Anytime you enter into an encounter with others, you are confronting their energy. Jasper works to cause all outcomes to be in one's best interest. This may not always be the thing one desires as the result, but, rather, what the cosmos sees as the best situation for you.

Jasper is applicable when going into job interviews, business presentations, and legal solicitations. When using the influence of jasper for legal confrontations, it is advisable to include amazonite which is for good judgment. The list of uses of this stone is virtually limitless.

Jasper is one of the stones that may be safely worn or used at all times as its function is to influence and not for detoxification as it is a shield stone. Regardless of your feelings about the elicited results, the presence of jasper insures that it is for the best. One of the first lessons we learn as children is that what we want is not always what we need.

Kunzite

Kunzite is for surrender.

When we speak of surrender, there is a vast spectrum of situations. When one finds himself in a living or working space that is unrewarding or unfulfilling, yet he must remain while pursuing or preparing for alternatives is one good example. In the course of losing a battle, such as a debate or argument, even to the point of having to call upon oneself to deliver an apology, kunzite is most helpful. Be mindful of the subtle differences in the two concepts of loss and surrender. The two are very close in nature. Refer to the material provided on rose quartz to determine appropriate applications.

Lapis

Lapis is to strengthen the spirit which is about you and for use in the spreads as a transmitter.

This beautiful blue rock is one of our most powerful influences and should always be used with the greatest of care. Often confused with sodalite, there is one sure way of determining its true family and that is by the presence of pyrite in the surface of the stone. This presence is more important, though, for its value emphasizing in an undeniable fashion, the importance of not setting lapis in any other metal than gold. It is so dangerous to put this stone in any other metal, that lapis itself, carries a constant reminder and indicator in its very appearance. It has always seemed incredulous to this author that with the obvious presence of the gold toned pyrite, how any intelligent person put lapis in silver. AS you refer to the safeguards associated with silver, you can see clearly the negative ramifications of this.

As stated, lapis will strengthen that spirit which is about you. This needs to be regarded very carefully, since one can have a spirit of anger, a spirit of sickness, a spirit of addiction, a spirit of depression, etc. Therefore, you must evaluate the spirit of one before opting to use this mineral. When used in proper combinations with the other two stones for female hormone balance, the lapis becomes altered to the specific application of the triad and poses no danger of abuse of giving strength to a contraindicated attitude or spirit.

The Ten Commandments were written on lapis. This is the stone which serves as a footrest at the throne of God, as described in the story of Moses' encounter on the mountain. The philosophers' stone also is of lapis. Many objects of spiritual antiquity were of this stone, although the description has been mistranslated and sapphire is what it has been called. In actuality, many translucent to opaque blue rocks were all called sapphire and ranged from true sapphire to lapis lazuli.

In application for female hormone imbalance, there is a triad of stones, as with the combination of three for male hormone imbalance. These combinations work as a team of three in each case, as well as having individual uses separate unto themselves. For female hormonal balance, we apply lapis, pearl and opal. The lapis is for matriarchal aspects which are inherent to the female physical, emotional, and spiritual system. This combination, as we've said, is a logical starting point for the use of Rock-Medicine in a woman's cleansing process.

When using lapis as a transmitter of long distance healing, the spread must be ringed with lapis. The strand used should be strung on non-metallic cord and would be inhibited by the presence of a metal clasp. This is, fortunately, not difficult to find, as there are many bead workers choosing this continuous method of stringing many stones and gems. (See section on spreads for specifics.)

There are very important safeguards regarding the use of this stone. First of all, is the obvious one of recognizing those times when the spirit is one that is not deserving of amplification. Secondly, is the danger of using lapis on someone who has latent emotional or psychological problems which can spontaneously surface, and the patient may not be ready or equipped to handle their onslaught. Lapis has a high saturation level. It can quite literally burn someone if used to excess. Recorded instances of rash or skin eruption can bear this out. If you find yourself having over-applied lapis, the antidote is the stone sugelite or louvelite, as it is also called. The application for most expeditious results would be an essence. When opting to use lapis alone, it is essential that you work up to it slowly by starting with only five minutes or so at first, and increasing the time frame of application slowly. Only the shield stones can be used for more than twenty minutes at a time in any given situation unless incorporated as preventative measures and deemed safe for constant application. When lapis is used with other stones it strengthens the spirit of them.

Lava

Lava is for command of authority.

This is one stone whose true use has been carefully guarded throughout the ages. It is for the safeguarding of the strong vibration of lava that all of the mysticism and superstition concerning the removal of pieces from the islands of Hawaii has been propagated. Even in these modern times, you can go to various museums and lava parks in Hawaii and find letters from literally every type of personality, from the most conservative to the most liberal. Their letters are of apology and to return the pieces they took. Many people are convinced that the lava brought them bad luck because they took it without permission or invitation of the goddess Pele.

This is a remarkable occurrence when you consider the aspects concerning volcanoes themselves. I'm sure you would tend to agree with me, that few things can command the attention of humankind like an erupting volcano. So, too, is it with the influence of lava. The key to it's use is the presence of some kind of authority having been bestowed in the first place. The range is quite vast. One may have authority over a classroom, an office, a project or committee, or even a country and its armies. Now, this could be a volatile situation. Lava does not distinguish between good and bad intentions on the part of the one who is seeking to better command his authority or position of authority. Just imagine if someone like Hitler had benefit of lava's power working on his behalf. Even greater disaster than what ensued would have been the result. This information is still to be used and guarded judiciously.

On the average level of application, one may use lava to be a better leader, guide, teacher, boss, and parent. When combined with other stones, such as herkimer diamond, you can exact a voice of authority or add red rock, as the author of this text did during writing, to produce the spiritual voice of authority.

Do not hesitate to use this wonderful stone, but exercise a reasonable amount of care in its application and know well your motives.

Lepidolite

Lepidolite is for brain chemical imbalance.

Often found as the matrix for pink tourmalines, this lavender stone is a lithium-based crystal and water-soluble. Therefore, it may not be used in an essence. The applications of this stone include hand holding, spreads, or focus direct.

The most obvious use of this stone is for manic-depression where there is a lithium imbalance. Any and all instances of brain-chemical disorder are treated with lepidolite. Head injury and brain contusion are two very important areas to include this element's influence and, likewise, for conditions of chemical dependency which call for the administration of lepidolite to balance the brain's chemical confusion. When the presence of brain infection has occurred in AIDS patients, lepidolite is included with the combination of stones for AIDS, as well as amethyst for the subsequent lesions and adhesions. The heavy use of various psycho tropic drugs by current medical practitioners has caused a high degree of residual toxicity which is counteracted by lepidolite. Comatose patients need lepidolite during the coma-state as a preventative measure for minimizing brain dysfunction. Pregnant women who are using prescribed drugs can use it to insure the brain-chemical balance in the unborn fetus, as well as for the infant post-delivery. The balance of the brain's chemicals is essential to proper mental function as we enter the age of more consciously using our mental powers.

Magnetite

Magnetite is for reversing the polarity of a situation.

This is a dramatic and extreme vibration. The applications are relatively few. This stone is the mineral equivalent to euthanasia. Magnetite is quite literally a "cure it or kill it" result. It is suggested that you do not opt for the application based on information, but rather, on a test of kinesiology to determine whether or not it is appropriate to use.

When a person has digressed to the point of deformity, and even if healed of the immediate disorder, would be left a dysfunctional individual, magnetite will release him from this realm. Two cases in point would be severely afflicted advanced cancer patients and accident/coma patients who have lost activity in vital areas.

The flip side to the use of magnetite is that in the course of grave illness, it will cause an immediate reversal of the injurious polarity. Magnetite is one of the fastest acting Rock-Medicine instruments! It has the potential to snatch one back from the grasp of death or catapult him into it.

One of the elusive imbalances of existence is suicidal tendency. To consider, on a conscious level, taking one's own life, takes both the utmost courage and daring, as well as the total failure of his survival instinct. This is a true paradox.

We have two types of suicidal personalities. One is the individual who merely desires attention and usually insures that he is rescued. If he dies, it is, more often than not, an accident. This group is not who magnetite is for. The second type is a tricky condition to recognize. This is the one who commits suicide to the astonishment of those closest to him. The soul who executes himself without giving any clear cut cry for help. It is by virtue of this thought process's nature to make the victim virtually unrecognizable. The opportunity to apply magnetite to these in need is usually after the interruption of a serious attempt. When in doubt, use it, because it is better to have it and not need it than to need it and not have it.

Remember, these stones are doing their job to the balance of things. They are programmed to seek their resonant vibration and see it to the highest level of well-being.

Malachite

Malachite is for the eyes.

This soft, green, banded, easily-carved stone is often found in copper mines and is a copper ore.

Proper vision on the mental and spiritual levels is what enables us to perceive a better world. This is the predecessor to enacting creative desires and making positive changes planet-wide. It is important to understand that the three bodies of existence--physical, mental, and spiritual--are inseparable. So, too, are the imbalances manifested in them. If you do not see correctly on the physical level, know that in correlation to that physical sight problem, the mental and spiritual visualization is off.

"Faithful" application means not missing any applications. Since Rock-Medicine works like antibiotics on a saturation-level of vibration, it is imperative that all uses of these methods be done as prescribed, without fail. It can take as little as three weeks on up to several months to correct stigmatisms, cataracts and other imbalances depending on their longevity, severity and the age of the patient.

Malachite is the stone in the sentence that denotes the area affected is the eyes. You would add the appropriate stones based on the other elements involved. Cataracts, for instance, is treated with a combination of the seven cleansers, amethyst for cell division and coral to indicate the presence of calcium deposits. For those situations where muscle weakness is the cause of poor vision halite is essential to the combination as is the seven cleansers. Rhodonite may be indicated if nerve damage or weakness is also present.

Not "seeing" properly is a contributing factor to many dangerous misconceptions and delusions. No one person's clarity of vision is more important that the next however, we can see where those in higher position of authority pose a greater threat to the health and welfare of the whole when they are without truth in their vision.

Remember that jade and amber are used with ALL applications of Rock-Medicine.

Moldavite

Moldavite is for all fungus-related imbalances.

Much controversy surrounds this relatively new mineral element which is not surprising since the area of resonance with which it relates is so elusive. While fungus extracts, penicillin for one, are being used successfully to treat many common maladies, they can be a threat as well. Moldavite is the stone of choice for such conditions as candida, skin fungi, (Tinea), and yeast infections. All of these have additional symptoms which call for the influences of other stones as well. Clay and smokey quartz are for the purification of body fluids, while rhodocrosite and amethyst are for skin-surface related fungi.

When evaluating the condition of fungal invasion, it is important to use the full spectrum of stones required.

Moonstone (Labradorite)

Moonstone (Labradorite) is for PMS-related syndrome and for regular monthly emotional upset. This white or pinkish chatoyant stone is one of the minerals commonly found in granite.

Men, as well as women, have dramatic responses to the moon's changing phases as it affects the individual metabolism. It is generally more evident in the emotions and behaviors of women. We call this Pre-Menstrual Syndrome (PMS). Along with the triad of stones for female hormone balance, moonstone is added to eradicate the disrupting effects of pre-menstrual stress.

Men may choose to use moonstone when they notice particular difficulty at certain times during their own monthly cycle of activity. In men, as we as women, it is not necessarily the same sequence of days that these effects are evident. Moonstone can be included in a daily-application essence as a preventative measure by both sexes. You may want to include petrified wood for emotional balance in extreme cases.

As the moon shines by the reflected light of our sun, it represents the analogy of women's reflective capacity for men's energies, and likewise, the matriarchal reflecting the patriarchal qualities. As we move into the matriarchal age, the cycles of changes will increase their intensity and protection by the moonstone will ease the tendency to overload.

The labradorite is the true moonstone. The common moonstones with the pale gray to white coloring are actually undergraduated star sapphires and are not to be confused.

Mother of Pearl

Mother of Pearl is for strengthening of the womb.

It is used for difficult or threatened pregnancies for those women who have a history of miscarriage or still births. It is suggested for use by those who are facilitating pregnancy in medically alternative methods, such as invitro fertilization. Late in lifers are always recommended to use it as it protects them-also because the health of the fetus is a direct reflection on the health of the mother and vice versa. It is actually wonderful that it can work that way.

In the event that a woman has required stitching to re-enforce the cervix, it is crucial that mother of pearl be applied.

This instrument is one of emergency measures when threat of miscarriage is present. This is especially for ill positioned uteruses and for cervical muscle weakness.

Obsidian

Obsidian is for prophecy.

This stone is volcanic glass and not a true crystal at all. Frequently black or grayish, there are varieties which have a silver or golden sheen just under the surface.

Prophecy, of course, is not a malady, but rather, a sometimes-desired condition by those seeking to tune-in to being of more assistance to the cosmic service corps. In the past, the choice to be one of those using the gift of prophesy has come due to the being's prior contract with the Creator before taking the earth-plane form. It sometimes surfaced spontaneously and without conscious preparation on the part of the individual. We are in times of great change as we mesh the cosmic consciousness with our own conscious capacity.

Obsidian does not create the gift of prophecy. If the gift of prophecy is present, obsidian hones and tunes it. If one desires the prophetic ability, the use of obsidian causes him to enter into a state of receptivity to it. Obviously, this type of work comes only after one has dealt with the presence of imbalances and maladies evident in one's existing state. Such is the case with red beryl for psychic development and jacinth for creative visualization.

Prophesy is the ability to act as the audible voice of things to come. This ability to look into the future serves many uses. We can better prepare for impending natural disasters, warn others regarding the dangerous effects of certain demonstrative actions, learn from negative attitudes without having the manifest them into reality. Most importantly, though, prophesy enables us to rest assured as to our guaranteed future heaven on earth so that it will serve to encourage others to facilitate its expeditious return.

The Creator's promise of salvation for his children is intact, and it is up to all of us as to whether we will have it sooner or later.

Onyx

Onyx shields from intense energy exchange.

Onyx is a two-way shield. Those who have intense energy at times may be unaware of the overwhelming effect that they have on the sensitivities of others. They would do well to protect their fragile brothers and sisters by wearing onyx to keep that energy contained. Likewise, the empaths and those among us with "open" chakras need onyx to protect against being inundated by the needy sponging of others.

It should be stressed that onyx, as with all stones, the use is determined by the need. Though you may view the list of available Rock-Medicine influences as entirely valuable, by no means are all the stones indicated for use by all.

Opal

Opal is for the elimination of fear or denial of one's divine calling.

All of the superstition surrounding opals throughout the ages is for good reason. They are indicative of the heavy influence the stone has with regard to the area of self-actualization. The elimination of fear and hesitancy to be our optimal level of existence is here.

Just as we have experienced delegation of authority and its abuses in the earth-plane, so now are we obtaining control and the usage of our individual authorities. Whenever there is motion of any kind in the universe, whether it be light, thought, or body that force has the first and singular point of impact, the leading edge so to speak. This position is the forefront of guidance. Opal represents the conscious decision to let go to the God-consciousness in each one.

Seeing one's pure potential has awed, fatefully at times, some of the greatest creative leadership to date. Many have burrowed away and hidden from the miracle they saw in themselves and the daring to dream such dreams of heavenly conscious existence. This present generation will bring it in. The influence of opal is the remedy for all peoples seeking to offer themselves in service to the spirit of well-being, and were afraid to ask.

Pearl

Pearl is for physical reproductive organs in women and for nurturing.

This beautiful luminous gem is one of the few formed in another living creature. Pearl is also the third in the triad of stones for female hormone balance. (The other two are opal and lapis).

When used as a single stone, pearl is a fortifier of the strength of the female reproductive organs. (This is not, however, the stone of choice for infertility). The utilization of pearl is as a general directive towards the reproductive system. If, for example, there are ovarian cysts, you would use the pearl to direct the influence of amethyst to the area for proper cell mitosis. This is what is meant by the use of pearl as a directive.

Procreation is the means by which we have populated this planet. For some, it is an effortless venture. For others, it is a tenuous balance of fragile imperfections of physical and emotional design. Men do not use either pearl or mother of pearl. It will not harm them. It is similar to the equation of peridot only being felt or effective in interacting with an enlightened individual. So it is that only women have a correlating band of vibratory rate equal to that of the one present in pearl. Mothers pass this energy influence to their sons as they nurture and feed them, thus working like mother's milk to send them out without requiring any further need for experiencing this aspect of vibration of the female sex. Such was woman's set assignment. Men and the patriarchal system are what gave the matriarchal guidelines their credence, when in the proverbial garden, he put the responsibility on the woman and NOT taking responsibility for his own actions. This set the danger tone to the previously existent patriarchal power seat.

Pearl, mother of pearl, and ivory are all stones used exclusively by women and all three are the product of a living creature. This is a fitting correlation of terms to that action which sets womankind apart from mankind, that of childbearing.

Man gave all things his name. Woman came out of the side of the man. This analogy is closely adhered to in nature for our constant awareness right up to our identification, in the nature of our culture. This author's lawyer-father gave her his best side that of "NOTHING IS MORE VALUABLE THAN TRUTH. What is.

The Philadelphia lawyer also held a degree in chemistry and one in physics. The third dimensional existence or number three is based upon the dovetailed existence of the mind, body, and spirit. The physical principles are aptly represented in our highest mind's knowledge of physics. The mind/brain is experienced to its potential through the course of study in chemistry and how it relates. This new age is the reintroduction of our spiritual awareness represented as that known as the law. As all things correlate in like, the technical utilization of law or spirit is just as orderly as that of equations of physics or chemistry. Change is constant, and, in that light, understand that it is the spirit of the change which gives that change its "nature". By this applied knowledge, we interject our nature or "spirit" out into the ever changing space around us and if our nature is to grow and be well as an individual, the changes around us will manifest those standards.

To be enlightened is to see the spirit of the creator in all things, or in other words, to see all things with love. If you have the presence of truth and that of self discipleship, there is unconditional love. The I AM. To seek perfection is to seek euphoria and total happiness. Happiness is "having all of one's needs met". This is a state of well being. The more conscious you are of the influences around you, the more educated you are. We are beings of study and application of knowledge to formulate wisdom or principles. Upon those principles, we based our "technological society". "Technology" is the term man popularly uses in the world today to describe that propensity towards his own creative nature when he first used a stone. Now we take our evolutionary step in the technological advancements of the spiritual science/studies and use them to create our heaven on earth.

Just as we have learned, by medical studies to date, to "communicate" with the physical existence (communicate meaning "exchange of information") and in the mental or academia existence, we have our numbers and letters to communicate with the spiritual energies (light energy). We have been provided, as is the way of nature, with more than enough information by way of the spirit, for us who set the divine order back into place. The work of making all things whole or one or holy, and we, ourselves, are transforming into the light beings from which this world came. This is realizing once again the existence of the personage of the Creator in each cell in us and about us. Human kind is entering the completion if the conscious awareness of the spiritual, mental, physical triad. It was the nature of man's separation of his will from that of the divine that the spiritual studies were called up by him at last. It was the nature of Love that made sure they were included at all. Love's existence on and in this planet is proof that there is a greater life of harmony existing elsewhere. Their visitations and interactions are well recorded. Only love breeds love. Only birds breed birds. Only a man and a woman produce a child. Therefore, we can see clearly by love's absence throughout our history that it has not been the focus of us as a people for all time so far. It was, however, left here in many ways by other intellects or conscious energies so that it could breed. The promise was also left with us that those energies would return to this place and join us to itself again. This understanding is shared by all except atheists (though they do not see that as being the case). This puts our conscious creative desire to seeing and interacting with all things as being dear to them as they are to themselves. Man and woman will see each other as "sister" and "brother" at all times.

The American band the Grateful Dead is enjoying a well earned success. They have been the phenomena medium by which the God consciousness known as LOVELIGHT (lovelight to the best of your capacity, the dance) came through in muse form in the sixties to gather the helpers set forth to assist the nations at this time of great change. The spirit of America, which is made up of all nations, is that of freedom specifically, the freedom of the individual. The American youths love movement. The sixties inspired at least two powerful forces--the common exchange of embracing one another and the celebration of that love in dance. At no time in history can we see anywhere since, the concepts of harmony, than rock and roll concerts and the dance.

The rainbow was set here and that which is awakening in each one of us. It is emerging as the symbol of the light age world it came from and the information it represents. Without light, there is no color. Where there is light, there is the presence of energy. We are earthbound creatures who evolved from water interacted upon by the light and produced organisms. The same dramatic level of change is upon us as it was then. Our natural and instinctive inclination is to be heavenward bound or skybound, whether warring or worshipping. All our environment's nature is to seek light. The physical applications are most evident. The mental spectrum includes those principles ranging from meditations and trances, to natural and processed hallucinogenics or chemical light. (What makes the heavens the heavens is the fact that is where the lights live and anyone can see that for himself.) The spirit, or inspiration, is fully upon us. The animal kingdom, man tainted, and he failed to tend the vegetable kingdom. Now we look into this new hope of the knowledge of practice of using the light energy producing crystals, gems, and stones which this mother earth has given birth to. We have a new age and baby new inhabitants of the mineral kingdom to complete a triad for transformation to light conscious beings.

The pearl is the capstone of Rock-Medicine. In its vibration we see birth of light energy in a physical form which produces a rainbow lustre. Its Essence is instinctive maternal nurturing wisdom, above price, breeding freedom from care. The matriarchal system, brought in by conscious presence of the holy spirit of love, is well represented in the "hen mothering" of constant care for her young being happy and satisfied and with a smile of satisfaction in their eye. This constant care rides a fine line for a tendency to be excessive. The matriarchal system was the birth of the exchange of men and women on the earth mutually involved in this process of creating a patriarchal system which its counterpart of "bride" could emerge from the "side" of. It is about having all things at one with their own individuality, and the wisdom to see that only in the nurturing with love the aspects of physical, mental, and ethereal practices can we prepare ourselves for THE GREAT EVENT by way of this GREAT WORK.

The pearl protects and sustains the womb of us all.

Petrified Wood

Petrified Wood is for emotional balance.

This ancient fossil of wood is one of the best tools for emergency measures. Use it for immediate relief of emotional upheaval, anxiety attacks, despair, feelings of helplessness, etc. Many physical emergencies worsen with stress trauma. Petrified wood, agatized stem tissue of trees, will balance emotional extremes and avert numerous cardiac situations.

The applications of this stone include, optimal, of course, hand held. It is a good addition to almost all essences, and is most helpful in long distance spreads. A variation on its usage is for pin-point application over short distances is a focus direct. To break up a fight situation or handle a trauma incident across a room, one needs a piece of petrified wood and a quartz crystal with a clean point. You must have a clear field of aim directly at the parties involved, with no one and nothing obstructing that directional path. Holding the petrified wood against the quartz, for focus and amplification, direct the stream of vibrational influence, which will be coming right out of the point (tip or tips) of the quartz, at your target. This practice is one of the most intensely dramatic displays of Rock-Medicine's capacities. Petrified wood is wonderful anti stress. So many illnesses and imbalances are the direct result of concentrated stress levels. This author suggests that everyone put a piece of petrified wood on a string around your neck

and wear it always against your skin.

Pyrite

Pyrite is for air purification.

Fool's gold, as pyrite is commonly called, is a very box like configuration. It is very similar to galena in appearance but for its gold color, where galena is silver cast. Pyrite is also a means of identifying lapis. Small flecks or veins of pyrite appear throughout most pieces of good quality lapis. It is the obvious indicator as to what the proper metal used in setting that stone should be (gold).

Pyrite is very beneficial to use in a spread where the presence of airborne pollutants is present. This can be either a private residence where there is a smoker living, or in a factory that has a form of production that lends itself to a toxic presence in the air. This includes global air pollution.

The combination of pyrite, white quartz, granite, iron, and clear quartz crystal may be used for full application for air pollution. The most effective method to use is a spread. The distance you are covering is related, of course, to the power of the amplification system (see spreads). This is a very important treatment worldwide and we need all the assistance we can get.

The man made pollutants were not here the last time divine presence visited this space. We must ready the air quality for its sake, as much as our own, since we are inseparable in the state of oneness. We have all the proof we need to concede that pollution of air and water is most detrimental to the health and well being of the mind, body, and spirit of the whole planet. Because of the severity of the pollution levels, our animal and vegetable kingdoms are in an extremely vulnerable position. Many necessary herbs and flower remedies are still needed as instruments, and yet are toxic themselves because of the total pollution of our environment. Efforts should be made to facilitate the use of hydroponics combined with sterile air conditions and true sunlight in order to provide the proper quality of these vegetable kingdom influences.

Pyrite may be used for the purification of lung air space, but is not the stone of choice. It is preferable that you use black tourmaline with watermelon tourmaline or in the form of rutilation inside a quartz. Use one form or the other, but not both.

Quartz

Quartz Crystal-Clear amplifies.

Quartz crystals amplify anything with which they come into contact, including thoughts, imbalances, wellness, other stones, etc. These simple mineral growths caught the children's eyes and started us looking at the value of beauty and enlightenment. Since they do amplify, there is a steady stream of misconceptions concerning their abilities.

Using a clear quartz, along with any administration of any vibrational work, will amplify the effort. Likewise, the influence of quartz on ailing conditions will amplify that as well. Clear quartz can be set to be any other instrument. To obtain these surrogate instruments, the quartz is placed to touch the source vibration. This source vibration can be a single stone, combination of stones or some essence water. The important points here are that the crystal touch the source and note that length of time. Once the clear quartz is physically removed from the source, it is the same as that particular energy, equally as strong, and for exactly the same amount of time as it touched the source. This is a wonderful remedy for the rarity of some minerals, their cost, and the highly domesticated need for obtaining quantities of Rock-Medicine tools.

The degree of amplification afforded by any given crystal or cluster is directly proportional to its size. The larger the clear crystal, the larger its parameters of influence. When using your clear quartz in long distance spreads, the more clear quartz you add, the greater the range of application. When using a clear quartz to send a point stream of another stone, the stones must be touching at the same time the crystal point is being directed at the person or persons being treated. This is also the case with mini-spreads. Whenever you pass the point-path of a clear crystal, which is touching other stones, you get "zapped" with a laser-like stream of energy. When a ring of lapis is added, that transmitter's influence changes the clear crystal to blanket application over the distance proportionate to the amount of amplification available.

A future function of clear quartz crystal is seen in our already strong penchant for wearing them as pendants about our necks. When clear quartz crystal is worn in a mineral-conscious community, it is a testimonial by the wearer that all is well with him that day. Should you not be well, it is recognizable immediately by all of us who love and are your wellness. We will have domestic health-care which is formatted towards preventative medicine, and the absence of your crystal would signify that help is needed. If, however, one should travel out imbalanced wearing his crystal, because of the very nature of the clear quartz, its function of amplification will quickly and ultimately surface the deception. Whenever feeling less than happy, healthy, and love, always take clear quartz crystals off. When you are wearing other minerals on your person the clear quartz crystal amplifies itself first, other minerals second, and only in the absence of other mineral's touch, will amplify whatever the given situation. (Note silver's influence.)

Quartz Crystal-Rose brings comfort and joy at times of sorrow over loss.

Rose quartz has been one of the first of the instruments of Rock-Medicine to be collected by the masses. This pale pink beauty has the nature of kindness in its vibrational influence. It works particularly well for those suffering grief over the death of a loved one. It will actually stop the hurt and tears.

Grief over loss is a much broader spectrum than one might imagine. Loss can be the loss of a job, home, or situation. Loss of a goal, a project, or an item of importance or value are all applicable here. Loss of a pet and children leaving home under the many circumstances by which this might occur are included, also. These are just some of the infinite examples of obvious loss.

An area that may not be so evident, is the loss of something that one has been reluctant to let go of for whatever reason. Some examples of this would be in the case of the loss of a bad habit or addiction that you have been consciously or sub-consciously holding on to. Two very common areas to apply this stone is for the loss of anger or a negative attitude. Anger is the way that the heart and mind defend themselves against hurt feelings turning to illness or despair. When situations occur in one's life, which cause disruption leaning towards hopelessness, this defense mechanism kicks in to safeguard the loss of self worth and manifests itself as anger because it is a more capable emotion to preserve the survival instinct than that of hurtful defeat. This is particularly true of interpersonal conflicts accompanying a romantic relationship.

Because the adage, "the truth hurts" is so often the case, we have this instrument of rose quartz to ease us through the difficult, yet inevitable, changes that occur in our daily lives. When we are corrected or criticized appropriately and our ego will not step aside for the input to be processed in a positively progressive manner, rose quartz will open up the appropriate receptors to facilitate the assimilation of necessary acceptance.

The best method for the use of rose quartz is the hand held method, since the use of this stone is so often an "on call" or as needed type of application. That is not to say the essence can't be used or is not effective, just that the use of the stone, itself, is the most expeditious manner to elicit immediate relief.

Quartz Crystal-Smokey is for water purification.

When we say that the smokey quartz will purify water, we are speaking both about external bodies of water, as well as the water content in one's body. Since we human beings are of a large proportion made up of water, this is a very good influence to use in the overall cleansing and balancing process using Rock-Medicine. This vibrational application is also well applied as an essence twice a day for a preventative to avoid toxic build-up as we work to clear the earth's bodies of water. You may put a piece of smokey quartz in a container of water and it will purify its contents so as to make it non-residual and non toxic for consumption. You must, however, begin with water that is relatively free from free floating pollutants or visibly dense impurities. It is possible to use smokey quartz in emergencies where the only water available is extremely tainted. It is better to use the stone and consume what water is necessary for survival.

In cases of kidney and bladder failure, the use of smokey quartz is imperative to decreasing the toxicity levels produced. All conditions of water retention including water on the brain and water on the knee or elbow need to be addressed by this stone, either as an essence or hand held application. Likewise, pustules such as water blisters and boils can be administered to by applying a drop or two of essence directly to the eruption.

Influenza is another area in which the smokey quartz will speed up the process of the body eliminating the malady, especially if the patient is consuming quantities of liquids as is the standard practice with flu and colds.

In order to treat vast areas of water like pools and ponds, the application would be to render an essence and dump it directly into the water. For the treatment of vast bodies of lakes and oceans, smokey quartz will be used in a wand or scepter apparatus which is constructed by specific instruction for amplification and focus. This type of instrument is one of the new instances where we are authorized to build crystal and gemstone mechanisms for large scale treatments. There are not many of these set-ups needed or authorized and must be used very carefully the main reason for this being the high power intensity of the nature of wands and scepters. For example, to point a wand apparatus, (not a fluorite), at an individual is like going after a small mouse with an atom bomb. That kind of force on an individual level is far, far too powerful and can easily cause damage. Wands are not to be taken lightly or used without specific understanding and instruction.

We are so far from the knowledge of the application of the influence of these instruments that they are not even included by the higher consciousness in this text.

Red Rock of Sedona

Red Rock of Sedona is an invitation to the Holy Spirit to come into one's midst.

It is otherwise known as Iko, call and response. The Iko-spirit is that of a ceremonious exchange with the Spirit of Light. In early African times, all that culture's dance offerings were preceded with the Iko. This word found its way through the slave trade to the Cajun area and its evolution of meanings has come full circle. With a contributing influence on rock and rhythm, it is the way to begin all gatherings and celebrations. It honors spiritual exchange.

The state of well-being is sustained by preventing harm or by preventative measures, therein comes provision, and as in all major celebrations, sending lots of invitations is a big part of the preparation. No wonder the red rock of invitation is so exciting, providing it and the knowledge to use it, is our own invitation from the spirit. We are preparing a place for a jubilee to occur, and it will manifest as do the preparations.

Used by one, it is a personal invitation to the Holy Spirit to come into his midst. When it is included in a long distance spread, it acts as a personal invitation by each and every person within its range. This invitation works the same for everyone, whether they want it, believe it, understand it, know it, or not. It is a very powerful good. Knowing to invite the holy spirit into our midst is an indication to us that it is already with us. This is prayer answered simultaneously with the request.

Rhodocrosite

Rhodocrosite is for epidermal tissue and growth of skin cells.

This pink-rose-white, soft, layered rock wears the clue to its use on its face. The flesh-pink banding and thin white lines aptly represent the skin tissue which this stone treats. Rhodocrosite can be used for everything from acne to tumors. The vast spectrum includes bites, boils, burns, rashes, eczema, seborrhea, psoriasis, endometriosis, skin grafts, incisions, abrasions, and various other injuries. Rhodocrosite with amethyst and lepidolite are essential elements in treating brain infections with resulting lesions and subsequent adhesions. They are also good for ovarian cysts and adhesions, as well as for treatment of malignant and non-malignant tumors.

Take care to include all pertinent stones for every intricate area of need.

Rhodonite

Rhodonite is for neurological disorder. Its' influence is on the electric body of our nervous system.

Our nerves carry fire and make our "body-electric". Nervous disorder manifests itself in a wide range of conditions involuntary movements on a chronic level, stuttering, narcolepsy, sciatic nerve, constantly self-conscious to a degree of embarrassment, base paranoia, just to name a few.

The manifestations of our nervous systems are like religion...as individual to one as his fingerprints. Of particular importance here, in dealing with the structure, messages, and awareness of the nervous system, is the true nature of the symptoms and whether they fall into the category of cause or effect. To use moderation or frugality in one's life is as a reverence to the availability of clean, pollution free existence. This means residual free, toxin free, and freedom from blockage of any sort. Free.

This condition known as lack of care is a neurotic one. It is traveling through the most sophisticated routing system imaginable. Single signals can be rapidly exchanged throughout the whole system in fractions of seconds. One of these signals gone awry can disrupt balance of patterning of many areas simultaneously.

The applications of rhodonite are perfectly suited for this "can of worms" type situation where there is no clear cut source of the malady(s) evident, and any form of nervous disorder is present. Most all psychiatric cases would be better served if the influence of rhodonite is administered, by hand or by essence, for at least three weeks before a conclusive evaluation is done for diagnosis and prognosis.

Ruby

Ruby is the physical, mental, and spiritual sex influencer.

Ruby derives its name from the blood red color of its appearance. It is one of the most dramatically changed stones from its former use to its current use, that of sexual centered afflictions. Let us begin, first, by stating that the application of ruby is not used in the treatment of AIDS, as AIDS is not the "sexual" disease it is being represented to be. The transmission of this disease has to do with the exchange of body fluids, primarily blood, and not the single element of sexual interaction, as with other so called sexual infirmities, such as gonorrhea and syphilis. Ruby is used for these two diseases, as well as in the treatment of genital herpes, male contraction of trichinosis, frigidity, inhibitions, and lack of healthy or adequate natural lubrication.

Some of the areas less often addressed from their sexual origins of aspect are recoveries from the traumas of rape, painful intercourse, and inadequate preparation by way of sex education. In observing these applicable situations, we see how the additional function of serving as a natural aphrodisiac is also one of the functions of the ruby. The application here is to touch the stone or a drop of essence directly to the skin surface at the point of the base of the spine. The misuse of the ruby as an aphrodisiac is a safeguard to be considered before adopting the practice. It is always preferable that the use of Rock-Medicine be with the knowledge of the patient. Obviously, in the event mental capacity is diminished or the patient is comatose, this is overridden. The application of ruby for opening the sexual stimuli channel is another instance where the awareness of the patient may not be desired. This is true when there is a lack of candid or comfortable communication between exclusive partners or spouses. Many people have great difficulty in verbalizing their feelings, fears, and preferences to each other when it comes to sexual intimacy. It is not acceptable to use ruby in this manner when it is merely to gain sexual favors of someone who is neither inclined nor predisposed to engaging in sexual activity with other than a designated mate. Treat this stone with respect.

Ruby is indicated in another area of sexual clarity and that is that of homosexuality, and the lack of one's clarity about their own sexual preference. Bisexual and homosexual tendencies and inclinations are not in themselves maladies. We are speaking exclusively about those individuals who remain confused as to their own desires and preferences, not those men and women who have made comfortable choices and decisions in these areas and are satisfied with their interpersonal interactions. You can rest assured that when any given situation doesn't feel right, something about it probably isn't. Likewise, when a healthy mind is happy and comfortable in its decision or condition, it is a good indication that the respective interactions are proper for that individual.

In the event the more severe syndromes of dangerous sado-masochistic behavior, necrophilia, nymphomania, and/or pedophilia is present, then you must surmise whether the symptoms are cause or effect. Only after this evaluation, can you proceed with the relevance of using ruby for the condition.

Selenite

Selenite is for childhood fears and traumas.

Selenite, a form of gypsum, treats the child's classic fears of the dark, dogs, nightmares, and bogeymen, but extends far beyond to cover the effects of abuse, incidental traumas, divorce, and death. We adult products of our childhood can use selenite to treat unresolved issues which occurred as children. We can also treat stunted growth patterns on the emotional and mental levels.

We are all children here, and we fight that aspect of our vulnerability. This condition is synonymous with the concept of time. Once life existed gracefully with nature and safe in the fabric of the time-space continuum. Then that fabric "tore" and it tore us away from the universal balance. We have been patching the hole that ill slips in through, for thousands of years. It is a cosmic band-aid. The weave is finally bridging the gap between mankind and Mother Earth. This will take us to a space where we may be so at one with our environment, that we can merge with it and its elements at will. These advanced practices will eliminate the wasteful means of travel and communications. Sounds like the dreams of children to me! Actually, it is science and mathematics and love's creation of a playground.

Sharks Tooth

Sharks Tooth is for the sinus and nasal passages.

Obviously, this is not a stone to be used by itself. You must give it some direction and guidance. In the case of allergies where the runny nose and watery eyes are present, a full combination to treat the body fluids and immune system, as well as general cleansing is used. If the allergy is due to pollen, dust, or anything of a particle type nature, you want to include the black tourmaline and watermelon tourmaline to clean off the interior of the lung surface. If the allergy has skin eruptions along with the sinus or nasal involvement, then rhodocrosite is added with amethyst to promote the skin's cell structure back to balance.

Of course, the common cold and flu would be treated with sharks tooth in addition to those other stones indicated for use. Understand that the sharks tooth in these two examples treat the symptomatic conditions in the nose and not the cause, itself. Other stones must be appropriately applied for this.

Any temporary or chronic smelling impairment or sensitivity is a relevant condition to treat with sharks tooth, also.

Silver

Silver causes all of the body's meridial, fluid, and energy flows to concentrate at the highest chakral point.

The highest chakral point is the topmost point of one's aura. This has been the case since the harmonic convergence since that time all the cells in your being from essence to aura are chakras. The literal topmost chakra point is the "highest" in all respects. It is physically located at the highest part of your being and is the closest in proximity to the higher consciousness.

First, we will address the safeguards to be taken into account when using silver. Silver is not conducive to being safely worn at all times, especially by women. The primary reason for this being the menstrual flow as a lower body elimination. Since the action of silver's influence is to raise all flows to the uppermost chakral area, its presence is contraindicated when the female system is attempting to send the monthly blood release to the lowest body orifice. This is certainly a contributing factor to those who experience cramping during this period. The body's attempts to pursue a downward flow are inhibited by the upward pull of the presence of silver causing conflictive energies and the resulting cramping in the middle body area. Another example of conditions which are acted upon counter productively by silver, in the body of either men or women, is the presence of bladder or kidney infection. This is again, the circumstance where the body's attempts at lower body elimination are inhibited by the upward influence of pull by the silver the danger being the constant reinfection of the already ailing area and ultimate weakening of natural healing instincts. Conditions resulting in the retention of excess body fluids of all types are all worsened by the presence of silver, either being held or worn by the individual. (This includes the use of real silverware used during a meal.)

This takes us to the question of proper use of silver. There is a vast number of situations where the concentration of energy flows is preferable for the highest chakral area. One such example is in the case of incontinence or lack of bladder control. The constant application of silver in this instance would quickly produce high levels of toxicity. However, for temporary protection from an embarrassing accident at a particular function or social event, one may use silver for a period of up to six hours to aid in his freedom from leakage or seepage. Likewise, in the event that a woman is at risk during pregnancy by either dropping too soon or losing her water, silver can be administered daily in the standard application of an essence to strengthen the conflict caused by the gravitational pull.

Silver is also an excellent choice for combining with any stones conducive to the higher studies to concentrate the thought processes of the mental and/or spiritual consciousness. One such use may be while using the hessonite garnet (jacinth) to promote higher visions of inspired quality, or when doing specific work with the chrysocolla for formal academic pursuits of a metaphysical nature. These uses are only for those times where the situations and conditions of safeguards have been observed.

At no time is lapis lazuli ever to be set in silver for any purpose. The reason being that the strengthening of one's spirit is a total being function and to concentrate this influential combination at the highest chakral point will very quickly "amp" out the conscious presence of mind and certain aspects of delusion and narcissism will result. (See lapis.)

The emotional attachment to objects worn of silver do not negate these standards.

Sodalite

Sodalite is for celebration.

Sometimes confused with lapis because of its blue coloring, it is generally softer than lapis (lapis can usually be identified by the presence of gold-colored iron pyrite). In using as stone whose influence is that of celebration, don't limit the possibilities. It is effective in opening the awareness up to the knowledge that Lovelight has got us all and everything covered...well-covered.

There can be a time when the joy, elation, and clarity can be so overwhelming, that one nearly faints. Believe me...it happens. When in the course of delighting in your work and gatherings and celebrations, increase the use of sodalite to give you more extension on containment capacity.

Sodalite is for when you feel the need to celebrate and when you've got so much to do you must have help staying on track to complete the work at hand.

Sugelite

Sugelite is for self-discipleship.

Self-discipleship is very close to self-control. The additional quality in self-discipleship is love. Love of yourself becomes synonymous with the love of all others, and the results create and ease in the daily dedication to see to the needs.

A very basic place to use sugelite is in individuals who are slack-natured towards healthy routine--people who have a tendency not to take, or not to take all, or not to take as directed prescribed therapies and medicines. This is particularly true of instances where the disease is not life-threatening or alarming enough to the patient.

Obviously, due to the nature of difficulty in administering to themselves, it is best to do a spread or put essence in all the beverage products in the house inclusive of safe consumption. This is not a stone to be used for extreme need only. We would all do well to have higher levels of true self-discipleship. This is disciplined and nurturing natures combined. It is an active dedication to a higher quality of life.

Sulfur

Sulfur is for inflammation and swelling of connective joint and muscle tissue.

This is the stone for arthritis and bursitis. It is used with halite in the treatment and prevention of atrophy in coma, paralysis, and geriatric patients. The standard application is to hold the stone directly of the skin surface of the afflicted area.

There are certain safeguards that must be observed in the use of sulfur and sulfite (they are inter-changeable). Due to the water-soluble nature of this mineral, we do not make an essence out of it because there would be residuals in the water. Sulfur must be kept off mucus membranes and open skin as it will burn it. This is an additional reason for not making an essence out of it or using it in a bath.

It is a valuable first-aid box tool for application to sprains and wrenchings. It is good assistance for whiplash injuries. It is used for the loss of muscle control, again with halite, in such conditions as muscular dystrophy. The full treatment of muscular dystrophy would include jade, amber, amethyst, rhodolite, halite, sulfur, smokey quartz, coral, hematite, clay, garnet, and gold.

Sulfur is brittle and fragile. Since the applications are always external, the handling of the stone can create much wear and tear. This is a good candidate for setting a clear quartz crystal to emulate sulfur instead.

Talc

Talc is for use during past-life regression work.

Talc is commonly used to make baby powder, bath powder, foot powder, and facial make-up powder. Talc is multi-dimensional in its prime role as the facilitator of past-life regression. This is not to be confused with rebirthings. It is strictly for past-life work and traumas. It is for clarity of facts and information. It adds comfort, ease, and protection during past-life trances. Talc does not bring one into a regressed state, but, rather is for help and clarity during such a trance state once induced.

On the mental and spiritual levels, it causes the past-life observations to convey strength and confidence in the knowledge that the real time has already occurred and the trance time is an opportunity for twenty\twenty hindsight. Past-life work is another exercise in acclimatizing us to the ideas of everlasting and infinite.

Tigers Eye

Tigers Eye is for fatigue.

It is not meant to replace needed sleep, but, rather to serve as a "shot in the arm" for those times when monotony and tedium set in. Tiger eye is used in the appropriate right or left hand and is held for ten to fifteen minutes. It gives an immediate energy boost, whether the need is physical, mental, or spiritual. Long waits, especially with children, and certainly traveling, are two excellent examples of standard use. At a long function or event, when you need a "second wind", tiger eye is most helpful.

It is a good stone to have on you for others and a great introduction to the use of Rock-Medicine.

Topaz

Topaz changes negative energy to positive.

We are not speaking of the electromagnetic concepts of negative and positive. It is the good verses bad that we mean. There are three stones everyone should have on themselves at all times. Agate, diamond, and topaz are the three. If it were possible to get only one stone in the hand of every individual, planet wide, at the same moment, if it were topaz we would have heaven on earth in an instant. This may sound like an impossibility, but I believe it is more easily accomplished than getting us all of one mind or belief.

There are three main colors of topaz. In terms of optimal use, the blue is for those in clinical or medical professions. The yellow is for those who teach and/or practice metaphysics. The smokey is for the general public. You may certainly use any color you like for yourself. This is just a guideline of optimal application for those in the first two categories.

Agate, diamond and topaz do not get toxic they are shields and can be worn constantly. One suggestion is to have an item of jewelry made with diamond and topaz in it, preferably in brass or gold. Remember that the size and quality of the stones is unimportant as long as they are true representations of their mineral family.

Topaz causes the negative or ailing vibrations at every level to be dissipated the void left is filled in by the surrounding opposite positive.

Tourmalines

Tourmalines do individual tasks based upon their individual colors.

Green tourmaline is for the treatment of blood sugar imbalance. It does not matter if the condition is diabetic or hypoglycemic. The green works to bring the level from either direction into balance. If a person is insulin dependent, it is required that diopside be added. It can't be reiterated enough times that you must set up a complete sentence when using stones. They refer to each other for directing their application. The jade, amber, hematite or carnelian for blood, and smokey quartz for water content are necessary when treating any blood sugar disorder. If glaucoma or kidney failure are threatened or present, use malachite in combination for the eyes or yellow calcite in a combination to indicate the kidney area. All of the combinations for the various maladies are not given in this book instead, sporadic examples are given for using the information to surmise what are proper and complete combinations.

Next is black tourmaline. This is for the lung's interior surface area. It is for removing or "scraping" foreign particles off the tissue and cilia. Some examples are found in airborne residuals from smog and air pollution. (Do not confuse the use of black tourmaline with that of rough fluorite, which is for fluid and mucus substances in the lungs. However, they may be indicated for use together.) Black tourmaline is applied in cases of black lung and other occupational or accidental circumstances where one has breathed toxic gasses, fumes, and irritant materials. On the other hand, if there is a deterioration of the lung interior surface area, this tourmaline builds it back up with the help of rhodocrosite and amethyst. It would be added to the combination for cancer when the lungs are involved.

Watermelon tourmaline is the gatekeeper for all the tourmalines. Pink tourmaline and watermelon tourmaline are the same in Rock-Medicine. The gatekeeper is needed because of the tourmaline's extreme nature in its ability to work in either direction. Watermelon, or pink, is what keeps the diabetic's sugar level stopped at the balance point and not continue on towards hypoglycemia. And, it prevents the black tourmaline from scraping the lung interior so harshly as to injure or remove the necessary cilia. It is suggested that those in the habit of wearing the green or black tourmaline get a pink, either set into the same piece of jewelry as the other two, or wear a separate piece of it at the same time. If there is no predisposition to blood sugar imbalance present, none will be created by the stones in any event.

Turquoise

Turquoise is a symbolic stone representing the wisdom of the ancients.

The currently active resonant tool for work or treatment in the area of knowledge and education is chrysocolla. Turquoise is in effect "retired" and serves as a reminder of all that humankind has endured and expedited to bring us to this point in time. It sits with the crystal ball as memorial opposed to instrumental. The crystal ball serves to remind us of the "all is one" reality.

Ulexite

Ulexite is for infidelity.

Ulexite combines with citrine and bornite for male hormone imbalance. When we speak of infidelity, we are not limiting our understanding of the word to marital arrangements. Infidelity is equally applicable to any situation where one is not being true to the family unit. The father who divorces and does not continue to pursue a full relationship with the children, the siblings who spend years on end in a grudge feud and don't live to make up, the daughter who disowns her mother and vice versa are all good examples. Use this stone any time a member of an immediate family unit, whether born of bloodlines or not, has closed the door of candid and healthy exchange or communication with other members of the unit. This is infidelity. Ironically, ulexite is also known as the T.V. stone for its fiber optic quality and appearance.

Wood Opal

Wood Opal is for the ears.

Whether it is the treatment of infection or the loss of hearing ability or even a mental listening block, wood opal is equally applicable when added to the proper Rock-Medicine sentence. Rock-Medicine is a form of science and will elicit amazing miracle-like responses in many cases. It is, however, a technology and does have its limitations. There are no examples where Rock-Medicine has restored vision to the blind or hearing to the deaf.

Some good applications are to those whose life puts them in situations where very loud noise is continuously doing damage. This can be music, machinery, or crowd noise. It is, of course, advisable to always act responsibly in engaging preventative measures, such as ear protection. Wood opal will work to improve any damage already sustained.

Many children, as well as adults, suffer from recurrent ear infection. When used with the cleansers, wood opal fights, as well as prevents, these infections.

In those who have trouble listening, you may want to employ the assistance of chrysocolla.

For use with higher level study, you might combine the red rock with the diamond and wood opal to set up a combination for hearing the voice of the spirit, or with sugelite to listen to your own heart's desires.

Wulfenite

Wulfenite is for extraneous trauma to the head area.

Any type of blow to the head is treated with wulfenite. Concussion, whether it is light or severe, needs wulfenite. This stone also works retroactively for treatment of old head injury.

Some specific examples of application are victims of accidents or abuse. Wulfenite prevents long term effects of swelling and bruising, as well as blood clotting and tumor. Wulfenite says "head" in any sentence you set up with it. Sometimes, you may need to include lepidolite for brain chemical involvement. As lepidolite works on the brain chemical imbalance, wulfenite works on the head, skull, and brain.

Anytime there is surgery in the head area, wulfenite is essential to the healing process. If the skull is involved, when you are treating tumors, whether malignant or benign, include white calcite. In the treatment of a chronic migraine headache, use jade, amber, and wulfenite. You may add chrysoprase for the pain as long as you know the cause of the headache. If that cause is stress, use petrified wood in addition. Remember the seven cleansers always.

Interpretation of the Cover

Interpretation of the Cover

This is presented by the artist, Peter Teekamp interpreting his 18 by 24 oil on canvas painting.

"I AM" stands for "GOD" the creator of the Universe

The "earth" is made of a thin layer of rock and water, like an "egg" filled with energy, floating in space

The "water" is a holy matter, full of life and wonder, used for healing, cleansing, and growth

The "heat" within the earth is the inner energy of light

The "crust" of the earth is made of rock with pressure and heat through time creates energy

> *Energy and water becomes love and light*
> *Love and Light becomes "healing"*
>
> *All that wonder is created by God*

To order an 11" by 17" full color print of this painting,
signed by the artist, please send:
$35.00 + $2.50 for shipping and handling

TO: Peter Teekamp
      1491 Sunnyslope Road #4
      Hollister, CA 95023
      408 636-2946

To order additional copies of this book, please send:
$21.50 + $2.50 for shipping (tax included)

TO: Lifeforce Publications
      1933 Hershner Drive
      San Jose, CA 95124

Index

blue calcite 11

boils 56

bone 32

bone damage 9

bone marrow 39

bornite 9, 11, 25

brain 9, 65

brain chemical imbalance 44

breaks 32

breastplate 40

brittle bones 32

broken bone 18

broken tooth 20

bronchial conditions 9, 35, 36

bruising 65

burns 9, 18, 56

bursitis 61

C

calcite 18, 25, 26, 39

calcium deposits 9, 32

cancer 10, 18, 25, 26

candida 10, 23

cardiac 10

carnelian 15, 23, 26, 27, 63

cataracts 9, 46

celebration 60

celestite 27

cell division 18

cervix 47

chakra 28, 59

chalcedony 27

chemical dependency 44

chemo-radiation 26

childhood fears 58

chronic back problems 34

chronic physical pain 29

chrysocolla 28, 65

chrysoprase 9, 10, 12, 27, 29, 65

cinnabar 10, 12, 26, 30

citrine 30

clay 23, 24, 31

cleansers 23

clear quartz xxiii

coal 31

cobalt 26

colds 55

command of authority 43

common cold 2

communication 64

complexion 10

comprehension 28

concussion 10, 65

congestion 35

conscious 28

coral 9, 11, 12, 20, 32, 34

covellite 22, 23, 24, 32, 33

creative visualization 40

cuts 10, 18

D

damage of tooth 19

damaged vertebrae 34

denial 27

dental 10

dependency 18

depression 10, 18

detoxification 18, 31, 40

diabetes 10

diabetic 63

diamond 33

dinosaur bone 34

diopside 10

divorce trauma 10

dizziness 37

DNA 17, 23

domestic maturity 14

domesticity 10

dream state 22

E

ear infection 64

ears 10, 64

eating disorders 10

eczema 56

education 28

egyptians 17

emerald 11, 12, 34

emotional balance 52

emphysema 10, 36

endomitrosis 10, 56

energy exchange 48

enhancer for the blood 36

epidermal tissue 56

epilepsy 10

essence 4

euthanasia 45

eyes 45

F

fainting 37

fatigue 10, 62

fear 10, 48

female hormone balance 10, 42

fever 10

first-aid 15

flu 10

flu 55

fluid 11

fluorite 9, 11, 12, 35

fluorite wands 35

fluorites 35

focus direct 5

food allergy 19

fool's gold 52

fossil 52

fossilized wood 27

freedom xxiii

frigidity 11

fungi 23, 46

G

galena 9, 10, 36

garnet 9, 11, 26, 36

gate 15

gatekeeper 63

general cleansing 11

gentleness 37

geriatrics 26

glaucoma 63

goiter 11, 33

gold 37

gonorrhea 57

good judgment. 16

granite 37

Grateful Dead 51

Great Work xxiii

green calcite 10

green tourmaline 10

grief 11, 54

gums 19

gypsum 58

H

habit 15

halite 9, 10, 11, 38, 46, 61

hallucinogenics 51

hand held 2

hangover 18

Harmonic Convergence 16, 24, 28, 30, 59

harmony 33

head 65

headache 11, 35

heart organ 30

heart surgery 30

heliotrope 9, 24, 27

hematite 18, 23, 24, 26, 38

hemimorphite 39

hemophilia 11

hepatitis 11

herkimer diamond 10, 11, 12, 26, 39, 44

herpes 11

hessonite garnet 11

HIV 24

holy grail 18

Holy Spirit 56

homosexuality 58

honey 9, 10, 18

hyperventilation 36

hypoglycemic 63

I

I Am 32

Iko 56

immune system 23, 31

impotence 11

indigestion 35

infertility 11, 40

infidelity 11, 64

inflammation 11, 61

influenza 55

injured gum 20

insect bites 2

insecurity 11

inspiration 11

invitro fertilization 47

iolite 32, 34, 39

irritability 11, 30

Itching 11, 30

ivory 11, 40

J

Jacinth/Hessonite Garnet 40

jade 23, 24, 40, 41

jasper 27, 41

jasper and onyx 27

jaw bone. 20

joint and muscle tissue 61

K

karmic 21

kidney failure 63

kindness 11, 37

kinesiology xvii, 45

kunzite 42

L

labradorite 46

lapis 42

larynx 11, 26, 39

lava 43

lepidolite 9, 10, 11, 12, 18, 44

lesions 56

leukemia 26

listening 65

lithium imbalance 44

lithium-based crysta 44

loss of hearing 64

louvelite 43

lung 63

lung fluid 35

M

magnetite 12, 45

malachite 9, 10, 45

male hormone balance 11, 25, 30, 64

manic-depression 44

masochistic 58

massage 38

master blend 8

meditation 36

memory stone 17

menopause 11

mercury poisoning 30

metabolism 33

metabolizing of nutrients 19

metaphysics xvii

methods Of Application 2

mica 12

migraine 65

miscarriage 47

moldavite 10, 23, 46

moldavite 10

molds 23

mononucleosis 11, 38

moonstone 46

mother of Pearl 47

motion sickness 35

mouth 19

multiple sclerosis 11, 17

muscle and skin elasticity 38

muscles 11

muscular dystrophy 11, 17, 38

N

nail biting 35

naked truth 27

narcolepsy 56

nasal passages 59

nausea 35, 37

neck injuries 34

necrophilia 58

negative energy 62

U

ulexite 64

ulexite 10, 11, 20

unity 20

V

vertigo 35

vision 45

visualization 40

vocal chords 12, 26, 39

W

wands 35

waste 12, 34

water pollution xxiii

water purification 55

watermelon or pink tourmaline
9, 10

weight 19

whiplash 39

white calcite 26, 65

white quartz xxiii

wisdom 28, 64

womb 47

wood Opal 10, 64

Wulfenite 10, 65

Y

yeast infections 23

yellow or orange calcite 10

Notes